T5-ANW-781

Breakthroughs in Family Therapy with Drug Abusing and Problem Youth

José Szapocznik, Ph.D, received his doctorate in Clinical Psychology from the University of Miami where he is presently Professor of Psychiatry at the School of Medicine. Currently, he is also Director of the Spanish Family Guidance Center, a post he has held since 1977; he also serves as Director of the Miami World Health Organization Collaborating Center for Research and Training in Mental Health, Alcohol, and Drug Dependence.

Dr. Szapocznik has received numerous grant awards from the National Institute of Mental Health as well as the National Institute of Drug Abuse. He is an active member of the American Psychological Association, National Coalition of Hispanic Health and Human Services Organization (COSSMHO), Society for Psychotherapy Research, and the National Hispanic Family Against Drug Abuse. He frequently lectures and gives workshops both here and abroad on family-oriented program development and minority mental health, among other topics.

William M. Kurtines, Ph.D., received his doctorate in Psychology from the Johns Hopkins University. He is Professor of Psychology and Director of Graduate Studies at Florida International University and a Research Professor of Psychiatry in the School of Medicine at the University of Miami, Miami, Florida. He is an active researcher in the area of family intervention and psychosocial development. Dr. Kurtines has published books and scientific articles on many topics in these areas.

Breakthroughs in Family Therapy with Drug Abusing and Problem Youth

José Szapocznik
William M. Kurtines
and contributors

SPRINGER PUBLISHING COMPANY
New York

616.8915
S996

Copyright © 1989 by Springer Publishing Company, Inc.

All rights reserved

No part of this publication may be reproduced, stored in a
retrieval system, or transmitted in any form or by any means,
electronic, mechanical, photocopying, recording, or otherwise,
without the prior permission of Springer Publishing Company, Inc.

Springer Publishing Company, Inc.
536 Broadway
New York, NY 10012

01 02 03 / 5 4 3

Library of Congress Cataloging-in-Publication Data

Szapocznik, José.
    Breakthroughs in family therapy with drug abusing and problem
youth / José Szapocznik and William M. Kurtines, and contributors.
       p.   cm.
    Bibliography: p.
    Includes index.
    ISBN 0-8261-6850-7
    1. Family psychotherapy. I. Kurtines, William M. II. Title
RC488.5.S98   1989   89-4206
616.89′156—dc 19   CIP

Printed in the United States of America

Contents

Preface

This is a book about family therapy—and more. This book is part of a growing movement to recognize the central role that families play in the lives of individuals—children, adolescents, adults. As such we assume that the lives of family members are interdependent. What sets us apart as family therapists is that we wish to maintain the interdependency of family members whenever possible. As family therapists our response to trouble is to look to the family for help. Our aim is, first, to identify those aspects of the family's patterns of interactions that are not letting the family (and its individual members) achieve its goals, and, second, to create the opportunity for the family to change these interactions, thereby preserving interdependency while exchanging unsuccessful interactions for more successful ones.

In the search for efficiency, effectiveness, and cost containment, whatever we can do to maximize the impact of an intervention by highly skilled therapists is welcome. As therapists we can spend at best a handful of hours with a patient. However, as change agents we can transform the family of a drug-abusing, problem youth into a therapeutic ally, and that family is likely to have many hours of contact, probably 7 days a week, 365 days a year, with that patient. This is one of the reasons for the effectiveness and expediency of family therapy in the treatment of a problem as difficult and recalcitrant as drug abuse. The therapist's role is to carry out changes in the family system that will bring about the kind of family interactions that will have a therapeutic impact on the youth—that is, that will influence the youth to change his or her drug-abusing behavior.

This book reviews structural family treatment of behavior-problem, drug-abusing youths and provides a detailed introduction to recent breakthroughs in the understanding and treatment of these youths. More importantly, the book is designed to provide professionals experienced in family therapy with a practical guide for using these breakthroughs in working with these youths, drawing on the authors' past 15 years of experience in the family therapy field. For more than a decade the authors have been developing and testing the treatment methods presented in this book. During the course of our work we have found that the most effective methods for treating drug abuse as well as related behavioral disorders are those that impact on the adolescent *and* the family system.

The effectiveness of family-oriented approaches is widely recognized in the research literature and by therapists who work with drug abusers. In a major national survey of 2,012 agencies offering services to drug abusers, 93% of the respondents indicated family therapy is the treatment of choice with drug abusers (Coleman & Davis, 1978). In our own work we have found that the most effective methods are those that (1) view drug abuse as part of a larger syndrome of behavior problems, (2) view the family as a system, (3) define a system in terms of repetitive patterns of interactions (labeled as structure), and (4) employ strategic methods for engaging clients in therapy as well as strategic and time-limited techniques that have maximum direct effect on family structure (i.e., interactive patterns). Taken together, these concepts and techniques make up what we call *Brief Strategic Family Therapy* (BSFT). This approach is useful in engaging families and resistant drug abusers in treatment, in diagnosing maladaptive family interactions (i.e., behaviors that are not helping the family achieve its objectives), and, finally, in helping us plan and implement change or treatment strategies.

This book is organized to highlight what we consider to be the most important breakthroughs that have come out of our work with families. Part I, "Systems, Structure, and Strategy," is an introduction to the conceptual innovations we have made in linking the concepts of systems, structure, and strategy. These concepts are at the core of our work with BSFT.

Part II, "Breakthroughs in Understanding and Diagnosing Family Functioning," covers the breakthroughs we have achieved in family assessment. We have found it necessary to go beyond conventional family therapy by developing and refining not only methods for treating families that need help but also maladaptive patterns of family interaction. We will describe our way of understanding families as structural systems and our novel diagnostic aids to facilitate the identification of maladaptive family structures that contribute to maintaining drug-abusing behaviors. The diagnostic aids described in Part II of the book enable the therapist to make rapid and accurate assessments of maladaptive family interactions.

Part III, "Treatment," describes the work we have done in further developing techniques for treating families that need help. These techniques represent a refinement of previously existing structural family systems therapy, such as that of Minuchin (Minuchin, 1974; Minuchin & Fishman, 1981), and the strategic approaches of Haley (1976) and Madanes (1981). To address some of the difficulties encountered with conventional family therapy, we have done extensive work on developing treatment methods that are both strategic (i.e., problem focused and pragmatic) and time limited. Family therapy can be difficult to implement when it requires engaging and retaining entire families in therapy over an extended period of time. Time-limited therapy, in contrast, is brief; BSFT is designed to be implemented in 12 sessions lasting about 1½ hours once a week. Limiting the number of sessions is one of the factors that contributes to the effectiveness of BSFT. Limiting the number of sessions not only makes it easier to engage families, it also gives the family the message that "we are here to work, and we intend to do it quickly." Part III will be devoted to providing a working knowledge and understanding of the application of basic BSFT techniques with the entire family.

Part IV, "Breakthroughs in Engaging Resistant Families," is designed to provide an introduction to some of the innovations we have developed for bringing resistant families into treatment. Although most therapists recognize the crucial role the family can play in treatment, most also complain that getting the whole family into treatment is typically improbable if not impossible. Coleman and Davis (1978), Stanton and his collaborators (Stanton, 1979; Stanton & Todd, 1981), and our own work (Szapocznik, Perez-Vidal, Hervis, Brickman, & Kurtines, 1989) have documented the difficulty of engaging and retaining drug abusers and their families in treatment. Thus although family therapy is widely recognized as desirable and effective in the treatment of youthful drug abusers, it has also proven difficult to implement.

In response to this challenge we have developed methods for getting into therapy families that might otherwise be lost to the treatment process. Unlike conventional family therapy, which views the treatment process as beginning once the family is in the therapist's office, we view treatment as beginning before the family gets to the therapist's office. For us the treatment process begins with the initial call for help from the client. Our approach teaches the therapist to view the treatment intervention as beginning with the first phone call or contact with the therapist. The focal problem—the therapeutic challenge—in the initial stages of treatment is to overcome resistance to therapy. Once families are engaged in therapy, the focal problem shifts from overcoming resistance to therapy, to the actual treatment. Because of the importance we place on overcoming resistance to therapy, we have developed a number of innovative and highly effective methods for using structural and strategic concepts for overcoming the initial resistance to therapy. Part IV of the book will provide the reader with a working knowledge and understanding of the techniques we have developed for engaging families in treatment.

Part V, "Working with One Person," goes beyond the most basic postulates of conventional family therapy, which assume that the entire family must be present in order to bring about change in family functioning. Although it is certainly desirable to have the entire family present, despite our best efforts to engage families there will be times when it is simply not possible to get the whole family to come into treatment. What is a family therapist to do? Part V provides the reader with an understanding and a set of therapeutic tools designed to accomplish the goals of family therapy while working primarily with one family member.

Part VI, "Research," presents a brief overview of research relevant to the three major topics covered in this book: diagnosis, engagement, and treatment. Part VI will review studies establishing the psychometric properties of our diagnostic procedures and the effectiveness of the engagement and treatment approaches presented in this book. The procedures described in this book were developed as part of four major clinical research studies, funded by the National Institute on Drug Abuse (Grant No. 1 R01 DA05334, Grant No. 5R18 DA0322, Grant No. DA02059, Grant No. 1 E07 02694) and the National Institute of Mental Health (Grant No. 1 R01 MH34821, Grant No. 1 R01 MH31236) for approximately $3.4 million (Szapocznik, Perez-Vidal, Hervis, Brickman, & Kurtines, 1989; Szapocznik, Perez-Vidal, Hervis, Foote, & Spencer, 1983; Szapocznik, Santisteban, Rio, Perez-Vidal, & Kurtines, 1984; Szapocznik et al., 1987). The results of this research have been previously published, in part, in primary journals and research reports (e.g., Szapocznik, Foote, Perez-Vidal, Hervis, & Kurtines, 1985; Szapocznik, Kurtines, Foote, Perez-Vidal, & Hervis, 1983, 1986; Szapocznik, Kurtines, Foote, Perez-Vidal, & Hervis, 1986; Szapocznik, Hervis, et al., under editorial review; Szapocznik, Rio, et al., in press).

Generally research is conducted to address one small problem at a time. However, important breakthroughs in knowledge development also require more than working on one small problem at a time. What is required is not only developing specific solutions to specific problems but also systematic efforts to integrate these results into the general body of knowledge available for use by practitioners in their daily clinical work. Thus the primary aim of this book is to make recent scientific breakthroughs in the understanding of family functioning and family treatment available to the practitioner.

Part I

Systems, Structure, and Strategy

1

Basic Concepts in Brief Strategic Family Therapy

A drug addict uses drugs repeatedly. We may say that he/she uses drugs compulsively. If we are person focused, we may attempt to understand the person and to develop therapies to help him change his behavior.

An apple falls from a tree to the ground. We pick it up, and as soon as we let it go, it falls to the ground again. Might we say that the apple falls to the ground compulsively?

In the case of the apple, to imply that it falls to the ground compulsively would raise questions about our sanity. Everyone knows about the laws of gravity—an invisible force that causes all objects to be pulled toward the center of the earth. The apple and the earth constitute a system, and as such they exert an influence upon each other.

While in the natural sciences the concept of systems is well established, in the behavioral sciences we are only beginning to understand and accept that groups of individuals constitute systems and that as such they can exert an influence on each other. Thus the behavior of a drug user may need to be understood in the context of the systems that exert an influence on the user, as much as the falling of an apple must be understood in the context of the pull of the earth's gravity.

From our point of view, it is as unrealistic to think of a drug user's behavior from an individual perspective as it is to imagine that the apple's falling toward the earth is controlled totally by its own properties and not at all by the interactive properties of the system comprised by the apple and the earth.

The purpose of this book is to illustrate the usefulness of a systems orientation in working with adolescents, with an emphasis on adolescents who present behavior problems, including drug abuse. Because the family represents, at least potentially, one of the most powerful systems influencing youth, the emphasis in this book will be on learning about the family system in relation to a youth's undesirable behavior.

This chapter introduces the essential concepts of Brief Strategic Family Therapy (BSFT): systems, structure, and strategy. These concepts are the basic building blocks of BSFT. The emphasis on systems and structures is derived from the theories of Salvador Minuchin (1974; Minuchin & Fishman, 1981). The emphasis on strategy is derived from the strategic theories of Jay Haley (1976) and Cloe Madanes (1981). But the work presented in this book represents our own thinking on strategic, structural, and systems concepts, as developed in our own family therapy work; while our work builds on the work of these other systemic and strategic theorists, it expands and extends their ideas in a number of ways. We begin our introduction to BSFT with the concept of systems; systems provide the context in which structural and strategic notions are considered.

SYSTEMS

We have all seen in our high school classes an experiment conducted with a magnet placed immediately under a sheet of paper. When iron filings are sprinkled on the sheet of paper (Fig. 1.1A), the filings move and organize themselves along invisible lines (Fig. 1.1B). What happened? The answer is that the iron filings were dropped into a magnetic field. The magnet and the filings constitute a system. When they get close to each other, they reveal properties or characteristics that were not apparent otherwise.

Similarly, a family is a system that exerts influence on all of its members. An individual (like an iron filing) may behave in a certain way when away from the family influence. However that same person reveals very different behavior when exposed to the invisible forces of the family system. The important notion that systems implies is that the family must be viewed as a *whole organism*—much more than merely the composite sum of the individuals or groups that comprise it.

FIGURE 1.1 Physical System

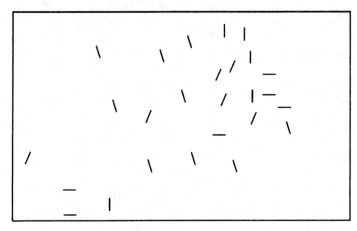

A: Scattered iron filings.

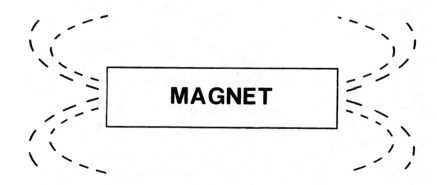

B: Iron filings under the influence of a magnet.

How does it happen that the whole is more than the sum of the parts? It happens because each family member behaves in a unique way in front of other family members. There are ways in which each one has become accustomed to behaving with each family member, behaviors that have occurred thousands of times over the many years that family members have been together and that have come to fit together like the parts of a puzzle—a perfect, predictable fit.

It is for these reasons that working with a person both individually as well as in the family context is so critical. As therapists, if we want to learn how an individual behaves, we must observe the individual also within the family context. Because the influence of the family system tends to be so incredibly powerful, it is not surprising that it becomes a gargantuan task for an individual to change when the family inadvertently exerts all of its powerful influence to keep the individual from changing. Conversely, the family's "power" is nearly irresistible when the family learns how to behave in ways that will cause an individual to adopt more adaptive behaviors. Typically, a family member, and particularly a child or adolescent, will readily "respond" to the family system's pull to behave adaptively (provided the family knows how to pull in the right way).

It is possible for some to escape the pull of the family system, but it is certainly not an easy task, just as it is possible to overcome the pull of the force of gravity, but it requires very powerful engines.

Because the forces of the family system are so difficult to overcome for a single individual, it seems to many of us that a more expedient way to bring about behavior change is to modify the family system so that its "new pull" will help elicit the new desired behaviors and also help maintain them; we thus consider the concept of system to have two significant implications for conceptualizing the individual and the family. The first is that *individual behaviors as well as behavior problems are identified as occurring not in isolation but in the context of the system in which the individuals find themselves.* Indeed, BSFT emphasizes that individuals and individual behavior can be understood *only* in terms of the context—the system and subsystems—to which the individual belongs. This means that in BSFT a holistic perspective underlies all attempts to understand the behavior of both the individual and the family.

The other major implication that the concept of system has is that *both family and individual behavior are viewed as interactive and interdependent.* That is, each individual's behavior, as well as interactions of the entire family system, is quite different from what it would be if it were possible for each individual to act in isolation.

This concept of parts of a system being interactive and interdependent has two important implications for our thinking about families. First, from a systems perspective, is that all individuals and subsystems contribute to maintaining the system's interactions. That is, they are *jointly* responsible for the current state of the family system as well as for any changes that are to occur. Second, for a system to maintain itself the behavior of all members must coordinate with and be contingent upon the behavior of others. In other words, they are linked. Technically this linking is called the *principle of complementarity.*

The principle of complementarity implies that for each action there is a complementary action. The behaviors of the members of a family are like the wheels that make up the inner workings of a clock. For the clock to keep on ticking, all the wheels must turn in a certain way. Similarly, for the family to continue to function or malfunction in a certain way, everyone's behavior must contribute to maintaining the family's pattern of behavior. The principle of complementarity further implies that behavior change in one part of the family system will force adjustments or changes to occur in other parts (i.e., other individuals) of the system.

STRUCTURE

This is the second fundamental concept of BSFT. The key phrase here is "patterns of interaction." While systems is a conceptually useful idea, in order to understand the mechanism through which a system operates, we need the notion of structure. We learned from the explanation of systems that behaviors between family members become linked in an interdependent fashion. In the vernacular, we might say that "they feed on each other" or that "they set each other off" or that "they trigger each other." These interdependent or linked behavioral interactions among individuals tend to repeat. In family members this repetition creates patterns of interactions. A large number of these typical *patterns of interaction* will evolve in any system—a friendship duo, a family, even a whole community. From the BSFT perspective, these repetitive patterns of interactions comprise a family system's *structure*.

When these family structures first emerge, they often develop because they are adaptive, as when a parent corrects a child's behavior through directive guidance. Directive guidance is adaptive in the case of the child's behavior because children may lack the maturity to respond to more nondirective methods. That is, these patterns of interaction work well for the family when they first emerge. Sometimes these structures become so ingrained that they become automatic. In these instances families are likely to use these automatic ways of interacting even in situations when they are no longer effective, as when directive methods of guidance appropriate for a child are used with an adolescent who is becoming more autonomous as a person. If this happens, it means that the structure is no longer functioning in a useful and appropriate fashion. Rather than being helpful and functional, the family structure has now become maladaptive.

In other cases structures that are never adaptive emerge when behaviors on the part of family members become linked in maladaptive ways.

For instance, a classic example of a triangulated relationship is the case in which a husband gets a piece of cake from the refrigerator, and his wife screams at him that he is going to kill himself by eating all of those sweets. Then the baby begins to cry and interrupts the argument. Should this pattern of interaction (child interrupts mother-father disagreement) tend to repeat itself with the same content as well as with different contents, we might say that it represents a rigidly repetitive pattern of maladaptive interactions that reflects an important aspect of the structure of this family.

At this point we have to address the question of what is adaptive or maladaptive. Defined in the family's words, maladaptive means that "we have a problem that is bothersome to us." We call this problem a symptom, and the symptom bearer is called the identified patient. This is not unlike the case of a person who comes to the physician because she or he has a high temperature or a rash. In either case the intelligent physician considers these symptoms of an underlying infection or allergic reaction, respectively.

When the family brings us a symptom, we redefine the problem in terms of what we as family therapists consider to be the problem. We redefine for ourselves that a problem exists because the family wishes to get rid of a problem and is not able to do so. Hence we define the dysfunction in terms of the family's inability to reach its own objectives of eliminating a bothersome problem. In our way of thinking, the family's inability to eliminate a bothersome problem is the cue that something is wrong. Our job is to find out what the family is doing to encourage and maintain the symptom. We assume that if the symptom persists then the family must be inadvertently doing something that keeps the problem alive. We also assume that the family could do something different that would eliminate the problem.

By definition an interaction for structural systems therapists is the "something" that the family is doing that maintains the problem and the "something" that the family could do differently to eliminate the problem.

Persistent problems of the kind that are brought to us as therapists are inadvertently supported by interactions that are equally persistent. In fact, we find that in families with problems, there tend to develop interactions that are repeated time after time in a rigid sort of way. Actually, it would be far more accurate to state the converse: Families in which certain interactions become repetitive in a rigid fashion are very likely to develop problems of the kind we call symptoms.

In BSFT, then, structure is a critical and extremely powerful concept that focuses on the interactive processes defining the way the family operates. The key to the BSFT concept of structure is that it is concerned with *the typical repetitive (habitual and probably rigid) patterns of interactions* that the family system has evolved.

STRATEGY

The third fundamental concept of BSFT, a strategic approach, means that we choose to be *pragmatic, problem focused, and planful* in our interventions. A bit of background will be helpful here. We adopted a strategic model because we wanted to develop an approach that was expedient—quick and effective in eliminating the problem symptom. In order to achieve this objective, we may need to be pragmatic in using strategies that work quickly, even though they seem unconventional; we need to be problem focused as a way of limiting the scope of the treatment; and, most of all, it is critical that we plan our interventions carefully.

"*Pragmatic*" refers to the fact that whatever techniques and strategies will work most effectively for the therapist are the ones that are employed. For example, at times the therapist may present perspectives that, rather than portraying the entire reality of a situation, present only those aspects the therapist wants to highlight, because they serve to move the therapy in a particular direction. For instance, in the case of a father who is berating his son for doing poorly in school, the therapist may choose to focus on dad's concern for the future well-being of the son as a way of building a bridge between dad and son. On the other hand, the therapist might have been more interested in establishing a bond between mom and dad and thus may have focused on how tired mom was of dealing with this problem, thus encouraging mom and dad to set up together rules on how to deal with son's poor school performance. In other words, the ultimate goal is to bring about a desired change in the interactive patterns; to do this, the therapist creates a new perspective or "frame" of reality—"reframes" the situation—and then uses this reframed reality to facilitate change.

The therapist uses whatever strategies are most likely to achieve the desired structural (interactive) changes with maximum speed, effect, and permanence. Note that this approach is radically different from an insight-oriented approach in which interpretations are made in an effort to have family members gain a greater and more accurate understanding of their behaviors and natures. In our strategic approach the therapist's interventions are not targeted at promoting greater understanding on the part of the family members but rather at *manipulating* the situation to promote desired changes in interactions.

"Pragmatic" also implies that the therapist concentrates her or his resources on interventions that will have maximum impact, in those areas of the system that the system is least able to change on its own. Some changes the family will be able to bring about by itself; some it will not, and it is the latter that become the therapist's focus.

"*Problem focused*" refers to the fact that BSFT focuses on changing those patterns of interactions that seem most directly related to the presenting problem, rather than targeting all potentially maladaptive interactive patterns. The energies and impact of the therapist are harnessed to bring about change on a particular "focal" problem, such as rebelliousness and drug abuse in an adolescent. If fundamental structural changes outside the immediate context of the focal problem are made, they are implemented only to the extent that they are necessary for a resolution to the problem.

Note that BSFT does not necessarily require a problem focus. It is possible for a family to present itself without a focal problem, though that is not typical. *Because most families imagine that their presenting complaint is really their main "problem," generally it is more strategic to use the presenting problem as a focus around which to create change.* This facilitates the therapist's access to the family and provides a ready rationale for engaging and maintaining the family in treatment. In this book we choose to present a time-limited, problem-focused approach because we believe it applies best to what most patients expect from their therapists (i.e., it is pragmatic). Except for this choice of being time limited and problem focused, the concepts and strategies presented in this book apply equally well to longer term, growth-oriented structural family therapy.

SYMPTOM

Now that we have talked about the basic building blocks of BSFT—system, structure, and strategy—it is also important to discuss the role and choice of the symptom. The symptom always presents itself as a problem behavior on the part of one of the family members. As already mentioned, one role of the symptom is to alert us about the family's inability to achieve its goal of eliminating problematic behavior that has come to be labeled a symptom. What the family often doesn't understand is that the problem behavior, while bothersome, continues to be maintained because it has an important function: perpetuating the family's pattern of interactions. A systems approach predicts such a circular path of causality, in which current events are interdependent among each other so that, for example, the symptom *and* the maladaptive interaction "cause each other" and "keep each other alive" (see Fig. 1.2). When the family tries to eliminate the symptom, its patterns of interactions also become threatened. At this point the family responds by attempting to strengthen its usual patterns of interaction, which paradoxically includes reinstating the symptom/problematic behavior.

Certain types of family interactions tend to give rise to certain types of symptoms. A family pattern of interaction involving the parents' inability to provide leadership and successful guidance and to set limits is likely to give rise to a syndrome of problem behaviors characterized by their acting-out nature. Thus it is not surprising that certain groups of problem behaviors/symptoms tend to occur together, because they result from a particular kind of family interaction. This syndrome of acting-out behaviors tends to include drug abuse. In our clinical experience as well as in research on acting-out behaviors, the "problem behavior syndrome" has been identified. One of the most influential researchers in this area has been Richard Jessor (1983, 1985; Jessor & Jessor, 1977).

The more basic process is found in the relationship between parents' inability to provide leadership, guidance, and directions and to set limits, on the one hand, and acting-out behaviors, on the other. However the specific kinds of acting-out behaviors of choice are influenced by conditions both within and outside the family. Such conditions may range from a family's culture to the norms of a society at a particular point in time. In these times in which drug use has been so prevalent, the behavior problem syndrome typically includes drug abuse.

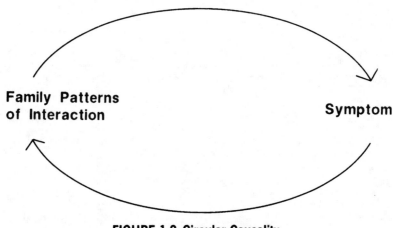

Family Patterns of Interaction

Symptom

FIGURE 1.2 Circular Causality.

Throughout this book the concepts, techniques, and strategies discussed tend to apply to the kinds of family interaction that give rise to problem behaviors. However, most of our cases were initially accepted into treatment because of their drug involvement. It should be made clear that in almost all instances we were treating those patterns in the family that gave rise not only to drug abuse but to the syndrome of which drug abuse was part.

Part II

Breakthroughs in Understanding and Diagnosing Family Functioning

Part II of this book delves into a deeper understanding of family functioning. In our strategic approach, expediency is achieved when we have a clear and detailed understanding of the family's structural organization and how it may be related to the family's presenting problem. Armed with such an understanding, the therapist can plan a treatment intervention with greater precision.

It is precisely for this reason that Chapters 2, 3, and 4 develop a strategy for analyzing the nature of the family's patterns of interactions, teach procedures for assessing and diagnosing maladaptive aspects of family interactions, and provide guidelines for what constitutes adaptive family functioning.

In Part II the complementary aspects of assessment and diagnosis are presented. First, an overall assessment of the adaptiveness of family interactions along the basic structural dimensions is proposed. Subsequently a diagnosis is made by identifying the relationship of the particular presenting problem to the type of maladaptive interactive patterns evidenced by the family; that is, the diagnosis is established by linking a presenting problem to the family's structure. Within this perspective it becomes evident that while BSFT is a problem-focused approach, it is always necessary to correct underlying maladaptive patterns of interactions that may influence the undesirable behavior, in order to increase the likelihood of permanence of the desired changes.

2

Understanding Families as Structural Systems

José Szapocznik, Olga Hervis, Arturo Rio,
William M. Kurtines, and Franklin Foote

A systems orientation helps us to understand the interrelation and interdependency fo family members. It reveals to us that, as the old adage goes, the whole is more than the sum of the parts. Systems helps us understand this phenomenon of the interdependency of family members and of the fitting together of the behaviors of the various members to construct a "whole" that is more than the sum of the parts. For therapeutic purposes, however, the generalities of a systems approach only leave us guessing as to how to proceed. It is for this reason

The material for this chapter was adapted from the Structural Family Systems Ratings manual developed as part of research projects funded by National Institute on Drug Abuse Grants No. 5R18 DA0322 and DA02059 and National Institute of Mental Health Grant No. 1 R01 MH34821.

that the concept of structure is so very useful, because it allows us to operationalize more precisely the nature of interdependency among family members. We have already discussed the concept of structure in a general way. Now we are ready to discuss in more detail how we can understand families as structural systems.

The question is of tremendous significance to therapists who are interested in behavior change because family systems therapists are not interested in changing the fact that family members are interdependent. Indeed, what makes us unique in the field is that we acknowledge, respect, and preserve the systemic nature of families. Rather, what we want to do is identify which aspects of its interactions (structures) are not working for the family and change them in such a way that new, more successful interactions emerge.

Thus structure is an extremely useful and important concept because it allows us to understand what is wrong or maladaptive within a family—that is, what kind of rigid interactive patterns are preventing the family from getting rid of their bothersome problem. The concept of structure also allows us to understand how a family may need to function or operate in order to be adaptive and successful.

The notion of the family structure—that is, the family's repetitive pattern of interactions—can be defined in many different ways. In our work we have found it useful to define family structure in terms of six interrelated dimensions: *structure, flexibility, resonance, developmental stage, identified patienthood, and conflict resolution.* These dimensions are at the core of the assessment and diagnostic procedures we have developed; we also use them to plan change strategies. We have defined along each of these dimensions what is likely or unlikely to be adaptive, although an important caveat here is that the adaptive range may vary according to the specific characteristics of each family, the cultural characteristics of each family, and the reality of the environment in which each family is immersed. Because these dimensions are central to our understanding of families as structural systems, we will introduce each one and describe the range of dysfunction associated with each. In later chapters we will describe in more detail how we use them to make structural diagnoses. It should be noted that the definitions provided below were developed for one- and two-parent nuclear families with children and/or adolescents.

STRUCTURE

We have already introduced the notion of structure. It is not surprising that structure is the first and central dimension that we want to understand. As mentioned, structure refers to the pattern of interaction. In assessing the structural dimension of family functioning, we want to examine three specific categories of family organization that can provide important and useful information regarding what might or might not be working in a family. These three categories are leadership, subsystem organization, and communication flow.

Leadership

This category is concerned with the distribution of authority and responsibility within the family. For this category the structural therapist is concerned with:

1. *Hierarchy*: Who takes charge of the family's directorship? Is leadership in the appropriate hands? Is it shared? Is hierarchy appropriate with respect to age, role, and function?
2. *Behavior control*: Who keeps order, if anyone? Are attempts to keep order successful or ignored?
3. *Guidance*: Who provides advice and suggestions? Does the advice provided have an impact on family interaction?

In functional two-parent families, leadership is in the hands of the parents. In modern societies such as ours, authority and decision making is usually shared by both parents. Frequently in one-parent families some of the leadership is shared with an older child. The latter is a delicate balance that can be functional, although it can easily become problematic as well.

Subsystem Organization

The second basic category of structure is concerned with the subsystems of the organization, both formal and informal. Their adequacy, degree of centralization, coalitions, and alliances are all relevant concerns. For this category of structure the structural therapist is concerned with:

1. *Alliances*: Who supports whom? Are dyad members closer to each other than to the rest of the family? Are alliances appropriate?
2. *Triangulations*: Are there triangulations within and across subsystems? (A triangulation is defined as an interference by family member C in a conflict between family members A and B, where C acts as an intermediary between A and B and where such interference causes a detour away from the original conflict.)

3. *Subsystem membership*: Who is a member of which subsystem? Are subsystems comprised appropriately as to age and function? Are subsystem boundaries clearly defined?

In functional two-parent families the primary alliance must be between the spouses, and this is particularly important around the issue of child rearing. Hence in front of the children the parents support each other, especially around child-rearing issues. In all cases alliances across generations (i.e., between a parent and one child) spell trouble because they blur hierarchical lines and undermine the system's ability to control behavior. Similarly, triangles always spell trouble because they prevent conflict resolution. Triangles occur when two authority figures are having a disagreement, and rather than resolving the disagreement between the two of them, they drag in a third, less powerful party to diffuse the conflict. Invariably this triangulated third party experiences stress and develops a symptom.

The subsystems in a family are usually defined along natural lines such that parents are a subsystem and siblings are a subsystem. These two subsystems in particular must have a certain degree of privacy and independence (i.e., boundaries). Boundaries, however, must be permeable and permit communication to come in and out. When these two natural subsystems are not clearly visible, exploration is likely to reveal some underlying problem that may be critical for overall family functioning.

Communication Flow

The final category of structure is concerned with communication flow within the family. Since successful communication is essential for overall good functioning, this dimension is also crucial. Here the therapist is concerned with the quality, quantity, and direction of all forms of communication within the family, especially with seeking to locate any communication blockages. It is important to examine not only formal systems but also the informal communication patterns that have developed. For this category the structural therapist is concerned with:

1. *Directness of communication*: Do individuals communicate directly with each other?
2. *Gatekeepers*: Is there a gatekeeper (switchboard operator) who controls, directs, or channels communication flow?
3. *Spokespersons*: Is there a family member who speaks for others in the family or for the whole family?

In functional families communication flow is characterized by directness and specificity of communication—the ability of each pairing of two members (dyads) of the family to communicate. For example, statements such as "I don't like it when you yell at me" are signs of good communication because the communication is both specific and direct.

The structural dimension defines the most basic aspects of the family's functioning. In our research on family functioning we have learned that the structural dimension accounts for most of the variance in family functioning. The remaining five dimensions, however, allow for a deeper and more detailed understanding of the nature of the interactions, particularly along an adaptiveness-maladaptiveness dimension.

FLEXIBILITY

Despite good leadership and authority as well as effective subsystem design and communication patterns, families that fail to respond well to the challenges of change—in other words, that lack flexibility—are impaired in their functioning. Indeed, the ease of restructuring is particularly affected by the level of flexibility in a system. Flexibility is one of the determinants of the amount of effort needed for restructuring (less effort with a more flexible family).

Circumstances, both within the family itself (e.g., birth, death, childhood developmental milestones) as well as outside the family (e.g., general economic or political changes, new technologies) change over time. The flexibility dimension partially reflects the ability of the family system to adapt to internal and external changes. In either case, to meet the challenge presented by change the internal family structure must change accordingly.

Flexibility is a measure of the family's ability to change and reorganize to meet changing needs or stimuli. A family exhibits more health as it shows its capability for shifting alliances and subsystem formation in an appropriate fashion so as to meet each task at hand.

To identify the level of flexibility, the therapist observes family change or reorganization in the following ways:

1. *Shifts in communication flow*: Do different members address other members as needed by the task or issue at hand?
2. *Shifts in alliances*: Do members freely support each other in response to the stimulus, conflict, or issue at hand, rather than supporting each other in terms of fixed roles within the family?

3. *Shifts in subsystem formation*: Do family members interact more intensely and/or cooperatively with other members in response to the task or stimulus at hand?

Flexibility is thus concerned with the appropriateness of shifts of communication flow, alliances, and subsystem formation in relation to family members' ages, nature of interaction, and changing circumstances. The therapist assesses the extent to which the family is able to reorganize itself to perform the different tasks.

Whereas flexibility is the sine qua non of adaptiveness, lack of flexibility or rigidity is the sine qua non of maladaptiveness. A family that cannot change will sooner or later not be able to meet new challenges and will develop symptoms.

A clear distinction should be made, however, between flexibility within a well defined structure and total lack of structure, which in itself is a form of rigidity because the family lacks the flexibility to create a functional structure. More specifically, some families tend to be so disorganized that systematic patterns of interaction have barely been established. These families, on the one hand, could be said to be eminently flexible. On the other, their excessive "flexibility" may be due to a rigidity of a different kind. This rigidity is manifested in the inability of these families to adjust by developing appropriate and adaptive interactive patterns. Instead they respond to most situations in a somewhat random and disorganized fashion. In a paradoxical way, then these families could be said to lack flexibility due to their inability to develop any kind of structure.

The differential diagnosis of the type of "rigidity" a family suffers is critical for the kind of intervention to be pursued. The rigid patterns of interaction in some families need to be changed. In disorganized families, however, treatment requires that some basic interactive patterns be developed, that is, that a minimum structure be established.

RESONANCE

Resonance is the sensitivity of family members to one another. An illustration is helpful in explaining the meaning of resonance. Imagine riding a car over a bumpy road. Various aspects in the design of the car, of which springs may be the most important, will determine how much of the bumpiness of the road is communicated to the passenger. Applying the notion of resonance to this example, high resonance would imply that whatever happens with the road is very clearly communicated to the passenger and the driver, and thus we would say that the boundaries between the road and the passenger are far too permeable. On the other hand, if the car was designed in such a way that the passenger could not feel anything of what goes on with the road, we would say that there is low resonance, or that the boundaries are impermeable (they don't let through the feeling of bumpiness).

Another analogy to depict the nature of resonance is found in the human cell. The human cell has an internal structure and set of functions and a membrane or boundary that defines the cell and separates it from the environment. The nature of the membrane defines the resonance of the cell. In the ideal case the membrane protects the integrity of the interior of the cell and yet is sufficiently permeable to allow an interactive process with the outside. If the membrane were not there at all, the cell's insides would "pour out." On the other hand, if the membrane were impermeable, the cell would perish because it could not receive its nutrients or excrete its toxins. Similarly, in the case of family members there is an ideal range of permeability that allows families and family members some "give-and-take" while maintaining their integrity.

Resonance, then, refers to the permeability of boundaries of subsystems (including those of each individual member). It may also be said that resonance is the emotional distance between family members. It is a measure of subsystem differentiation that takes into account the threshold of each family member's sensitivity to the others. At one extreme, boundaries can be either extremely rigid or impermeable; this is called *disengagement*. At the opposite extreme, they can be too permeable or almost nonexistent; this is called *enmeshment*. Both of these extremes are maladaptive and result in less functional structures that give rise to problems.

Ideally there is a midpoint that allows for permeability such that interaction and communication is possible at appropriate times, while retaining adequate differentiation and separateness.

The following are examples of the types of behaviors the therapist looks for in determining the family resonance level. For the first set a high frequency of occurrence indicates a high degree of enmeshment. The second set of behaviors reveals the existence of disengagement. The final section on resonance presents a continuum of adaptiveness in terms of the quality of differentiation of responses.

Enmeshment

Mind Readings
One family member speaks for a second family member, saying what the latter believes, wants, or feels without this second family member's expressing an opinion, or else the latter's verbalizations are overridden.

Mediated Responses
In these responses one person acts as a pathway for two other persons (e.g., person A tells person C what person B means or wants), or one person attempts to make another person such a pathway (i.e., person A tells person C or asks person C about something that person B, who is present, said). These responses are always a sign of triangulation and thus reflect maladaptive interactions in this dimension as well as in the structure dimension.

Simultaneous Speeches
Two or more people talk at the same time for more than a few seconds.

Interruptions
One person breaks into and stops another's speech on a topic or train of thought different from that of the original speaker.

Continuations
One person breaks into or enters into another's speech with some sense of logical and grammatical continuity with that of the original speaker; there may be a brief overlap when both are speaking simultaneously, or the original speaker may have paused without completing the thought.

Personal Control
Person A speaks authoritatively about person B to person C in a way that implies person A has special knowledge about person B or control of person B (e.g., "Person B usually likes gravy with his potatoes."), or person C asks person A a question which implies that person A has such control of knowledge. Personal control is differentiated from mediated responses and mind readings on the basis of this sense of authority, control, and power.

Loss of Distance
Two or more people getting very close together or touching each other in a manner meant to control, silence, or intimidate one or the other or both.

Joint Affective Reaction
Crying together, laughing together, or some other emotional, nonverbal expression by two people together, frequently as a temporary replacement for verbal communication.

Engagement Reaction
A chain or series of interchanges, such as teasing, joking, arguing, or discussing, that spreads from one dyad to another, often distracting from a task or causing degeneration into circular discussion or overly involved detail.

Disengagement

Emotional Distance

Person A presents or relates some feeling or emotion, and person B continues to behave as if no such feeling or emotion has been presented.

Behaviors reflective of disengagement principally involve claims that a given family member is not to be involved ("Oh, he doesn't care"), needs to be protected ("Let's not bother him" or "He is far too busy to attend sessions"), or similar claims by the disengaged family member(s). Other behaviors also reflective of disengagement are attribution of responsibility to others instead of to self ("That's not my problem; it is theirs").

Level of Differentiation

In addition to the occurrence of the behaviors described above, the therapist must also be alert to their *quality*, defined in terms of the *degree of differentiation* of the responses of the family members. The types of responses the therapist looks for include (listed on a continuum from adaptive to maladaptive):

Differentiated Responses

Refers to that healthy category of behavior wherein a particular family member is spoken about in terms that are clear, unambiguous, and somewhat unique to that person. For example, "John is a good student; he always gets good grades" or "Suzy never helps to clean the table."

Semidifferentiated Responses

Some grouping of family members, but not the entire family, is stated or implied (e.g., "You kids never pick up your toys" or—child to parents—"Why don't you two get off my back?"), or the content of the communication about an individual is somewhat vague (e.g., "Person A is immature," without giving more specifics). These semidifferentiated responses are not optimum but are not as unhealthy as undifferentiated responses.

Undifferentiated Responses

Family members are referred to not as individuals but as a class or part of a larger group. The content is somewhat ambiguous and nonspecific, although there may be some differentiation between family subsystems (e.g., "You [children] misbehaved" or "You [parents] are always angry").

In assessing resonance using these behaviors, the therapist should always be sensitive to the context in which they occur in relation to family structure, task accomplishment, and conflict resolution. In addition, some allowances must be made for the cultural background of the family. For example, traditional Latin/Hispanic families naturally tend to have more permeable (enmeshed) boundaries than white American families; white American families, in turn, may have more permeable (less disengaged) boundaries than Oriental families.

While certain allowances are made for cultural differences, when behaviors result in symptoms, we consider them problematic whether or not they are culturally sanctioned. Thus even when a behavior is culturally sanctioned, if it results in problems, we wish to explore how to facilitate a change—while acknowledging respect for it and its usefulness and significance within certain cultural frameworks. For example, a certain amount of simultaneous speeches, interruptions, or continuations may be acceptable in a Cuban family, but not if these result in interference with resolution of a conflict, serve to undermine parental authority, or serve to promote a maladaptive coalition. Thus when behaviors interfere with adaptive functioning, they are assessed as maladaptive even if they reflect cultural trends. Conversely, when a behavior is sanctioned by culture, even if it appears atypical, we do not assume it to be maladaptive.

DEVELOPMENTAL STAGE

All professionals in the mental health field have learned human development from an individual development point of view. Thus individuals are expected to go through a series of developmental stages: infancy, childhood, adolescence, young adulthood, middle age, young old, and old old. We have learned that certain conditions, roles, and responsibilities may typically occur at each stage.

Families also move through a series of developmental steps, and at each developmental stage family members should behave in ways that are appropriate for the family's developmental level.

The earliest stage of development is when two people first meet. At this time all of the attention of the couple is on each other. The next step may begin when the couple begins to expect a child and the first child is born. At this time the attention tends to be redirected from the spousal couple to the child. A subsequent stage occurs when a second child is born and the attention once more is shifted to incorporate this second child. Other major milestones come when the children grow from infancy to childhood and begin school, when the children reach adolescence and begin to claim greater independence, when the children begin to leave home, when the last child leaves home and the spousal couple find themselves "alone," when one or both partners retire, when one of the partners dies, and at any time throughout the chronological sequence if the spousal couple separates, and one of them leaves the nest. Other less predictable developmental milestones may involve the death of a child or the serious illness of any family member. Events in the extended family may constitute yet other milestones, outside the nuclear family but affecting it.

Each time a developmental milestone is reached, the family must adapt to the new circumstances. Failure to adapt, to make the transition, to give up behaviors that were used successfully at a prior developmental stage in order to establish new behaviors that are adaptive to the new developmental stage, will cause the family to develop unwanted symptoms in family members. Thus behaviors that were adaptive at one time become maladaptive when circumstances change. The family's flexibility—ability to adapt—will clearly impact profoundly the family's ability to adapt to new circumstances, including new circumstances caused by developmental shifts.

The appropriateness of the family's behavior in terms of its developmental stage can be most readily assessed by observing the appropriateness of family members' interactions in terms of roles and tasks assigned to various family members, taking into consideration their age and position within the family. There are four major sets of tasks and roles to be assessed: parenting tasks and roles, spousal tasks and roles, sibling tasks and roles, and extended family tasks and roles. If the household includes extended family members (e.g., grandparents, aunts, uncles, etc.), then the functioning of these members (are they taking over the role of parenting? Sabotaging the parents? Given too much parental responsibility?) must also be considered. Careful judgments are needed in determining the appropriateness of interactions, especially with regard to the children. In making this judgment the therapist should take into account the family's cultural heritage.

The following sets of roles and tasks should be considered in examining this dimension:

1. *Parenting roles and tasks*: Are parents parenting at a level consistent with the age of the children? For example, are controlling and nurturant functions in accord with a child's age and stage of psychological development?
2. *Spousal roles and tasks*: Are spouses parenting at cooperative and equal levels of development?
3. *Child/sibling roles and tasks*: Do the children function competently for their age and have appropriate rights and responsibilities?

4. *Extended family members' roles and tasks*: In extended families, are parents able to assume the proper parental position relative to their children, in light of the role of their own parents and other relatives?

It is noteworthy that the major flare-ups in family stress and conflict are likely to emerge at times when developmental milestones are reached, because these occasions expose the family to unexpected, stressful demands. Frequently, as the family attempts to deal in old ways with the new emergent situation represented by a developmental milestone, crises develop that force the family to seek help.

IDENTIFIED PATIENTHOOD

Identified patienthood refers to the extent to which the family is convinced that their primary problem is *all* the fault of the person exhibiting the symptom, who is variously defined as the identified patient or the symptom bearer. This dimension is an excellent measure of level of pathology and prognosis. The more the family insists that its entire problem is found in a single person, the more difficult it will be to bring about change. On the other hand, the family that acknowledges that various family members may have problems is far more flexible and healthier, and throughout the therapy process bringing about changes in such a family will be easier—relatively.

The reason we can use identified patienthood as a prognostic indicator is that the family that uses a single person as the only receptacle for all of its blame will find it most difficult to move to a stance where it will consider or accept changing the family interaction patterns. The family systems therapist believes that the problem is in the family's repetitive (habitual, rigid) patterns of interactions. Thus the family systems therapist will not necessarily aim to change only the identified patient (IP), but rather the interactions in the family that are causing the IP's noxious behavior (or its perception that the behavior is noxious) to persist.

Identified patienthood (or IPhood) refers to the extent to which the family considers the IP and her or his identified problem to be the sole problem of the family and uses that IPhood as a means of maintaining family homeostasis (i.e., the current balance). There are five symptoms indicative of strong IPhood:

1. *Negativity about the IP*: Statements are made to the effect that the IP is the sole cause of family pain and unhappiness.

2. *IP centrality*: The IP is frequently the center of attention and topic of conversation and interactions.
3. *Overprotection of the IPhood*: The family avoids confrontation with IP dysfunction by excusing it, explaining it away, minimizing it, or feeling that there is nothing that can be done about it ("That's just the way she is").
4. *Nurturance of the IPhood*: The IP dysfunction is supported or abetted by other family members; for example, a sibling does the homework for an IP getting bad grades.
5. *Denial of other problems*: Statements are made implying that the IP is causing problems and pain, coupled with statements that there are no other family problems ("We would be a happy family if it wasn't for this problem").

One sign serves to ameliorate the severity of the IPhood: statement(s) by family member(s) that identify another member (other than the IP) as someone with a problem or with some type of symptomatology—for example, "Joe is very disobedient, and his sister can also get me very angry sometimes."

The existence of a second IPhood indicates that the family is capable of recognizing other problems rather than focusing solely on the IP and the presenting complaint. This moderating variable is extremely important in ascertaining the degree of maladaptiveness of family functioning along this dimension.

CONFLICT RESOLUTION

Conflict resolution is a measure of the family's ability to express, confront, and negotiate differences of opinion, disagreements, and conflict. It is important to observe the handling of differences and disagreements in a variety of situations, since various situations, differing in the level of inherent conflict or level of emotionality, may be handled differently. Each set of disagreements is placed into one of five conflict resolution categories:

Denial
Conflict is not allowed to emerge. Situations are structured to avoid different opinions or critical opinions, or redefined to avoid the emergence of conflict. For example, each person is assigned a separate role or portion of a task, and no alternatives are called for; or one person might do all the talking, with others only allowed to agree or not disagree; or as soon as one opinion is expressed, there is instant

agreement; or there is denial of conflict or disagreement, even to the extent of not doing the task—for example, inability to give critical opinions of others even when required ("I can't think of anything" or "There's nothing I don't like").

Avoidance
Conflict begins to emerge but is stopped, masked, or strongly inhibited in some way: "Let's not have a fight now," "You're so cute when you're mad," "That's not really important," "It would be no problem if we had more money." "Objective" reasons (rationalizations) are offered for the conflict, or statements are retracted to avoid the conflict. Members react to conflict with humor or ridicule, or may simply refuse to talk about it, or global solutions are offered that place the blame for a conflict on variables external to the family.

Diffusion
Avoiding or sabotaging clear emergence and confrontation by going from one conflict to another without letting any emerge fully or by making personal attacks that are not part of the conflict issue.

Emergence Without Resolution
Separate accounts and opinions regarding one conflict are clearly expressed and confronted, but no one account is finally accepted and no solution negotiated.

Emergence with Resolution
Separate accounts and opinions regarding a single conflict are clearly expressed and confronted, and a single final version or solution acceptable to all family members is negotiated.

It should be noted that cultural differences may affect what kind of conflict resolution style is most prevalent. Certain cultures, for instance the Oriental, are more likely to deny conflicts; others, such as the Cuban, are more likely to diffuse conflict; yet others, such as psychologically oriented mental health practitioners, are more likely to value full conflict emergence.

There is considerable debate as to which of these conflict resolution styles is most adaptive and successful. From a family systems, communication theory, and psychoanalytic point of view, it might be possible to order these conflict resolution styles from least to most healthy, as follows:

1. Denial
2. Avoidance
3. Diffusion
4. Conflict emergence without resolution
5. Conflict emergence with resolution

However, from a more strategic perspective it can be suggested that different styles may be adaptive at certain times. For example, a couple that felt compelled to fully discuss and negotiate to resolution every difference that emerged would find themselves spending an inordinate amount of time and energy in this endeavor. A more adaptive strategy would be to prioritize what are important differences and what are less important, and to choose which sets of differences are sufficiently important to the adaptive functioning of the system to warrant full discussion and negotiation. In this case, negotiation of nonimportant differences would be avoided for the sake of giving priority to the negotiation of the most important differences. As strategic therapists we adopt precisely this kind of an approach, in that we prioritize the conflicts that may be important to resolve and at least temporarily make other conflicts subservient until our target conflict has been resolved.

There are also particular times when certain conflict resolution styles may be particularly useful. For example, crisis specialists suggest that a good dose of denial for the period immediately following the aftermath of massively disastrous situations may actually be highly adaptive. Similarly, we have all encountered instances in which diffusing a conflict may be adaptive by preventing a breakdown in communication.

It is for these reasons that while we recommend a general rule for assessing conflict resolution along a continuum from pathology to health, we also recommend exercising considerable judgment in determining what is an appropriate mode of conflict resolution given the overall circumstances confronted.

THE SYMPTOM AND THE UNDERLYING PROBLEM

Systems theory teaches us that family members are interdependent. As family therapists we believe that some aspects of this interdependency cause some families to develop bothersome behaviors we call symptoms. In order to define explicitly the aspect of the interdependency that can cause problems, we have identified and defined six characteristics of families' patterns of interactions. We have further postulated, based on our clinical experiences and those of other structural therapists such as Minuchin (1974) that understanding these six dimensions is both *necessary and sufficient* for diagnosing in any family the interactive malaise that is encouraging and maintaining the problem symptom.

For the family, the presenting problem or symptom is their ticket to coming to therapy; for the therapist, diagnosing the maladaptive aspects of the interactions is crucial to developing and implementing a treatment plan. The diagnosis of a problem must always consider both the general family/structural functioning and the presenting problem's relationship to general family/structural functioning. No matter what the presenting problem is, an essential first step is to structurally assess and diagnose the family's overall functioning. Essentially, the presenting problem needs to be placed in its proper context since it is only a symptom of broader, more pervasive structural/interactive maladaptations.

The next two chapters provide examples of how the understanding provided by the six structural dimensions can be applied to the diagnosis of family malfunctions. Throughout our work we have found that planning treatment requires having a good road map of how the family functions and what about its interactive patterns has to be changed. It is for these reasons that we developed a standardized procedure for assessing family interactions. We find our family assessments and diagnoses akin to a surgeon's X rays or laboratory tests: They not only help reveal the nature of the problem causing the symptoms, but they also considerably increase the precision of interventions, thereby making the interventions faster, less intrusive, and certainly less painful.

3

Assessment and Diagnosis: The Family Tasks and the Structural Family Systems Ratings

*José Szapocznik, Arturo Rio, Olga Hervis,
Franklin Foote, and William M. Kurtines*

Just as effective treatment rests on accurate diagnosis, accurate diagnosis rests on reliable assessment. In this chapter we introduce the *formal* assessment procedures that we have developed to facilitate making accurate diagnoses and discuss less formal ways of arriving at a structural diagnosis. Assessment pertains to gathering information; diagno-

The material for this chapter was adapted from the *Structural Family Systems Ratings Manual* developed as part of research projects funded by National Institute on Drug Abuse Grants No. 5R18 DA0322 and DA02059 and National Institute of Mental Health Grant No. 1 R01 MH34821.

sis pertains to drawing conclusions about the meaning of the information gathered. Diagnosis involves using assessment information to make decisions about which interactions are maladaptive and should be changed. The assessment procedure that we developed provides the foundation for our diagnostic work. We strongly recommend that you familiarize yourself with the formal assessment procedure. Even if you don't use it in your own work, it will provide you with a solid foundation for using a less formal procedure for obtaining this information. We will describe how to use the norms and concepts from the formal assessment procedure to make clinical, less formal assessments at the end of this chapter.

The assessment procedures we will describe in this chapter have both clinical and research uses. Clinically they are used to diagnose the nature of the interactional problems, and for research and evaluation they are used to measure the nature and impact of a treatment intervention on family interactions by administering it before and after therapy.

The formal assessment procedure has two parts: a set of standardized stimuli called the *Family Tasks*, and a rating system called the *Structural Family Systems Ratings*.

The Family Tasks are a set of standard stimuli initially developed by Salvador Minuchin and Bernice Rosman (Minuchin, 1974). The Family Tasks are specifically designed to elicit family interactional patterns along the six family interactional dimensions described in the previous chapter. Because above all we are interested in learning how the family functions when it is alone, without the interference of a therapist, the Family Tasks provide an *in vivo* exercise in which the family is placed in a situation and encouraged to interact "naturally." The family is asked to interact by itself—and hence without the interference of a therapist in the room—by responding to three simple standardized and structured situations. This strategy is likely to provide far more relevant clinical material than responses to a paper and pencil test in which the family members report their perceptions and not their actual behavior.

The Structural Family Systems Ratings (SFSR) is a set of six rating scales designed by the authors of this chapter (Szapocznik, Foote, Perez-Vidal, Hervis, & Kurtines, 1985; Szapocznik, Kurtines, Foote, Perez-Vidal, & Hervis, 1983, 1986) specifically to clinically evaluate the family's responses to the Family Tasks along the six structural dimensions, noting structural, systemic aspects of family functioning and pathology. In addition, a total score measuring overall family pathology can be calculated from the sum of the six scales and used to evaluate the overall level of the family's functioning.

We think that the SFSR has a number of advantages that highlight its usefulness to the clinician. One of the most important advantages is that it is a diagnostic procedure that is fully integrated with the clinical work described throughout this book and fully compatible with structural family therapy and theory.

A great advantage of SFSR is that it is highly efficient in terms of administration time (approximately 20 min) and scoring (approximately 15–20 min) when conducted by an experienced, trained clinician. Such efficiency represents a remarkable advantage.

The SFSR has been designed both for diagnostic and treatment evaluation purposes. As a diagnostic tool it provides an assessment of the maladaptive interactional patterns that need to be addressed in treatment; as an evaluation tool it is sensitive to changes that occur as a result of treatment (Szapocznik et al., 1983, 1986; Szapocznik, Kurtines, Perez-Vidal, Hervis, & Foote, in press).

Finally, from a theoretical point of view the SFSR has considerable heuristic value because it clarifies the relationship between specific categories of family interactions and structural concepts, both clinical and theoretical. Thus *it provides a mechanism for initiating the investigation of the relationship between specific categories of family interactions and clinical problems*. Data collection for the SFSR is based on a standardized procedure that yields numerical values lending themselves to straightforward statistical analyses and interpretations.

STRUCTURAL FAMILY SYSTEMS RATINGS: THE FORMAL PROCEDURE[1]

Why spend time making formal assessments when assessment information can be gathered informally? One compelling reason is that the availability of more objective and accurate information that formal assessment makes possible results in more accurate diagnosis. Formal assessment increases the precision of the diagnosis, reduces overall length of therapy, and, last but certainly not least, it provides accurate information on how the family operates, which can be used to increase the precision and effectiveness of interventions. From a research standpoint it greatly increases the reliability of the ratings.

The first step in the administration is to ask the family members to interact with one another on the three standardized Family Tasks: (1) deciding on a menu for a meal, (2) telling what pleases and dis-

---

[1]For the reader interested in the research application of the Structural Family Systems Ratings, information pertinent to its research applications and psychometric properties is found in Szapocznik, Hervis, et al., (under editorial review).

pleases them about other family members, and (3) describing the most recent family fight or argument. The clinician conducting the assessment then uses the information from the Family Tasks to rate the family on a form that uses specific categories of interactions initially adapted from the work of Bernice Rosman (personal communication, 1976). This clinical information on the categories of interaction is then used to rate the family's functioning along six Likert scales, each assessing one of the six basic dimensions of family functioning.

We will separate our discussion of how to use the SFSR into two sections. Section I will give a basic description of how to use the Family Tasks and the SFSR to make a formal assessment and diagnosis. The SFSR form used in making the formal assessment is provided in the Appendix. Section II will explain how to conduct a less formal assessment and diagnosis, for use in clinical practice.

I. HOW TO ADMINISTER THE STRUCTURAL FAMILY SYSTEMS RATINGS FOR A FORMAL ASSESSMENT

Instructions for the Family Tasks

All psychometric procedures used in diagnosis and assessment, such as tests and measures, start with standard stimuli. Responses of different individuals (or families) to the same stimuli can then be compared to help us determine how the persons responding are alike and how they are different in their responses to the same standard stimuli. The SFSR is no different. The SFSR is used to assess how families function along each of the six structural dimensions in response to the standardized Family Tasks. To ensure a standardized stimulus, the instructions for the Family Tasks should be tape-recorded, and the tape-recorded task instructions should be played to the family, one task at a time. The therapist or individual conducting the evaluation introduces the Family Tasks during the initial or admission session, as follows: "Let us now move to videotaping the family evaluation. These are three tasks that you will perform as a family. The directions will be given to you via the cassette player, so please listen carefully. You have five minutes to complete each task."

First, Task I is played for the family. When the instructions for Task I have been completed, the family is left alone and given 5 min to respond. After the family finishes the task or the time limit has elapsed, the second task's instructions are played, and the family is again left alone for approximately 5 min to respond, and similarly for Task III. If a family asks the interviewer for clarification about the directions for a particular task, the taped directions for that task should be played again. No elaboration, explanation, or examples should be given. Do not help the family by explaining the task!

Our colleagues have raised the question of whether the 5 min per task time limit should be fixed or flexible. Our experience has been that the basic information is obtained in 5 min for most families. Larger families (five or more members) may require several more minutes in Task II (and possibly III), but 10 min is generally more than sufficient time for 98% of all families. We have found that tasks lasting more than 10 min do not add sufficient information for the rating to warrant the extra time required by the family, task administrator, or rater.

We have also been asked whether the family should be reminded that they only have 5 min at the end of the directions for each task. Our experience has been that families who are given a 5-min time limit for each task become anxious or pressured and thus tend to rush through the tasks and not perform in a natural interactional fashion (i.e., as they would behave at home). We therefore recommend that families not be reminded of a time limit before or after the directions for each of the tasks.

The recordings of the three tasks should be as follows:

Task I Planning the Menu
"Suppose all of you had to work out a menu for dinner tonight and would all like to have your favorite foods for dinner, but you can only have one meat, two vegetables, one drink, and one dessert. Talk together about it, but you must decide on one meal you would all enjoy that has one meat, two vegetables, one drink, and one dessert. Remember, you must end up agreeing on just one meal that everyone would enjoy. Okay, go ahead."

Task II Things Others Do in the Family That Please or Displease You
"Each of you tell about the things everyone does in the family: the things that please you the most and make you feel good, and also the things each one does that make you unhappy or mad. Everyone try to give his own ideas about this. Go ahead."

Task III A Family Argument
"In every family things happen that cause a fuss now and then. Discuss and talk together about an argument you had—a fight or argument at home that you can remember. Talk together about it: like what started it, who was in on it, and what went on, and also how it turned out at the end. See if you can remember what it was all about. Take your time. Go ahead."

Converting Clinical Observations into Ratings: The Structural Family Systems Ratings

This section provides detailed instructions for scoring each of the six SFSR scales: structure, flexibility, resonance, developmental stage, identified patienthood, and conflict resolution. In order to conduct the ratings, the rater should know which member of the family has been designated as the IP and the family role of each member, such as mother, father, aunt, sister, and cousin. This is not a problem when the therapist is doing the ratings for their clinical diagnostic value only, because the therapist will know who the various family members are. However, when an independent rater is used (which should be the case when these ratings are used for the research evaluation of treatment outcome), the rater should be told who the IP is and the role of each family member, but have no further information. For a formal research evaluation, ratings should be based on all the information that can be gathered as the family executes the Family Tasks but should *not* be based on events that occur at any other time (including anything they might say or do as they enter the room just prior to beginning the Family Tasks or in between the tasks).

These restrictions are not needed when ratings are conducted for clinical purposes only, in which case the procedure need not be so strictly standardized. In our own work our preferred way of conducting a clinical assessment is to conduct the Family Tasks in the formal way, including audiotaped instructions and videotaped responses. Then we either observe this material through the one-way mirror or we review the videotape later. We like videotaping because it allows us to review the material when needed: several times, periodically, or occasionally as therapeutically useful. It may also be used later to show to the family or selected members.

With regard to scoring, for each of the six scales there are a number of specific interactional categories to evaluate. Moreover, behaviors that occur during each of the three Family Tasks may be scored in more than one scale and/or interactional category. In such cases the same behavior will be scored in each of the categories it represents across the six scales. The rater should score the event on all categories that it impacts. For example, if mother interrupts a child during the menu planning and says that the child talks too much and that she—the mother—has decided that the vegetable is going to be peas, that event may impact the scores for the structure, resonance, developmental stage, and conflict resolution scales and, if so, should be marked on all four scales. This means that for most families the rater will have to view the videotape of the family tasks several times, marking the interactional categories for only two, or at most three, scales on each run-through.

We remind the reader once more that an important issue is the cultural fairness of the ratings. Interactions should always be evaluated within the cultural context of the family engaged in the tasks. Several people talking at once, for example, has varying degrees of significance in Hispanic, American, and Japanese families. On the other hand, if a behavior impacts on conflict resolution, task accomplishment, or structural functioning, then it must be scored as less functional even if it is a cultural norm. This concern requires that the rater be very familiar with the cultural background of the family being rated. Special attention to this concern is noted for some of the scales described below.

What follow are explanations, definitions, and detailed descriptions of how to rate each of the six scales. Because these dimensions were outlined in detail in Chapter 2, we will only review them briefly here. Our main concern will be how to convert the clinical observations into ratings. It will help you to understand these ratings if you have a copy of the SFSR form (App.) as you go through them.

Structure

Structure is a measure of the manner in which interactional patterns yield a specific family organization. Structure variables are grouped into three general categories: leadership, subsystem organization, and communication flow. These three categories and their corresponding variables are defined below.

TABLE 3.1 Variables

Leadership	Subsystem Organization	Communication Flow
1. Hierarchy	1. Alliances	1. Directness
2. Behavior control	2. Triangulation	2. Gatekeeper-switchboard operator
3. Guidance	3. Subsystem membership	3. Spokesperson

Structure should be rated on Tasks I and III.

Task I elicits structure material in a nonstressful climate. Task III elicits material under stressful conditions. Task II is usually not as relevant for the measurement of structure because there is relatively little interaction, since family members usually take turns in completing the task.

Ratings are based on the following descriptions of anchors for the structure scale:

"5" *Highly functional structure*: At least two of the three structural components of the system are rated excellent, and the other one at least an average level. Subsystems are formed along appropriate age, role, and function lines and are not invaded by triangulations. Mechanisms for behavior control and guidance exist, are effective, and are in the appropriate hands. Hierarchical lines of authority are appropriate with respect to age, role, and function and are not crossed-over. Communication is always dyadic; there are no gatekeepers or switchboard operators. Everyone in the family has free communication access to everyone else, and it is used. Power is balanced within the executive system and effectively used. By effective use it is meant that tasks (e.g., leadership, nurturance, decision making) are accomplished successfully.

"4" *Good structure*: Reasonably well functioning systemic organization with some minor flaws. The flaws do not impede effective and appropriate system behavior.

"3" *Average structure*: Generally healthy structure but there is at least one major flaw that impedes some major aspect of family and/or individual functioning. Examples of dysfunctions are only one parent exercises behavior control; one child is left out of communication more than the others; some alliances may be inappropriate, though not seriously damaging to system functioning; power may be somewhat unbalanced in the executive subsystem.

"2" *Maladaptive structure*: While there may be a few healthy aspects, family structure exhibits at least two dimensional flaws. For example, communication may be through a switchboard, thus isolating and alienating some members from others; one child may be carrying out parental role(s) and be hierarchically positioned above the parent she/he is substituting for; a child may be triangulated in the parental subsystem; necessary alliances along expected subsystem lines do not exist.

"1" *Very maladaptive structure*: The family structure is clearly very unhealthy. All three major dimensions are rated dysfunctional. For example, neither parent has authority in the family; one parent is allied with a powerful child, and it is an alliance that attacks the other parent; parents do not communicate with each

other; any one member is left out of communicati
system participation; alliances cross appropriate si
triangulations exist; subsystem membership is ina

Flexibility

Flexibility is a measure of the family's ability to change and reorganize to meet changing needs or stimuli. A family exhibits more health as it shows its capability for shifting alliances and subsystem formation in an appropriate fashion so as to meet each task at hand.

To rate this scale, the rater observes not only possible changes (shifts) within each task but also the system's shifts from task to task. Family change or reorganization is rated for the following variables:

TABLE 3.2 Variables

Flexibility
1. Communication flow shifts
2. Alliance shifts
3. Subsystem formation changes

Flexibility refers to the family's ability to handle and resolve conflict in a fashion other than fixed use of rigid automatic denial or outright avoidance (see conflict resolution scale). Also of particular importance are those shifts that support or create an appropriate structure to meet a particular task at hand.

The flexibility scale thus assesses the appropriateness of the family's shifts in communication flow, alliances, and subsystem formation in relation to family members' age, nature of interaction, and changing circumstances.

Flexibility is rated on all three tasks, since the rater must assess the extent to which the family is able to reorganize itself to perform the different tasks. The final rating is obtained by calculating a percentage of the number of appropriate shifts as a function of the total number of shifts that occur throughout the three family tasks: appropriate shifts divided by total shifts and multiplied by 100. The following anchors and descriptors are used in arriving at a flexibility rating:

"5" *Very flexible*: Appropriate shifts occur successfully at least 90% of the time.

"4" *Moderately flexible*: appropriate shifts occur successfully at least 75% of the time, but less than 90% of the time.

"3"   *Somewhat flexible*: Appropriate shifts occur successfully at least 50% of the time, but less than 75% of the time.

"2"   *Moderately rigid*: Appropriate shifts occur successfully at least 25% of the time, but less than 50% of the time.

"1"   *Very rigid*: Appropriate shifts occur successfully less than 25% of the time, or less than two shifts occur.

Resonance

Resonance is a measure of the permeability of boundaries of subsystems (including those of each individual member). It is a measure of subsystem differentiation that takes into account the threshhold of each family member's sensitivity to the others. At one extreme, boundaries can be either extremely rigid or impermeable (disengagement). At the opposite extreme, they can be too permeable or almost nonexistent (enmeshment). Both of these extremes are maladaptive and result in less functional structures, which give rise to system dysfunction.

Ideally there is a midpoint that allows for permeability, such that interaction and communication are possible at appropriate times, while adequate differentiation and separateness are retained.

The following variables are assessed in determining family resonance level. For the first set of variables the rater observes the frequency of occurance of these variables as indicating a high degree of enmeshment. The second set of variables is rated for disengagement. The third set of variables is rated for degree of differentiation.

TABLE 3.3 Variables

Enmeshment	Disengagement	Differentiation
1. Mind readings	1. Emotional distance	1. Differentiated responses
2. Simultaneous speeches, interruptions, and continuations	2. Protection of a member's distance	2. Semidifferentiated responses
3. Personal control (implied power over other family members)	3. Member not seen or does not see self as part of the family problem	3. Undifferentiated responses
4. Loss of physical distance		
5. Response differentiation (ranges from differentiated to global)		
6. Joint affective reactions		
7. Engagement reactions		

It should be noted that in the experience of the authors and their collaborators, many families where one member was disengaged also revealed other members who were enmeshed, and hence it was the discrepancy of the emotional distance between members that revealed an imbalance. Thus in many of our cases families tended to show both enmeshment and disengagement at once (enmeshment among some members while others remained peripheral). However other possibilities may also occur, such as families where all members are enmeshed or all members are disengaged.

To score the resonance scale, the raters need to pay particular attention to Tasks I and II, but primarily to Task II.

Ratings on this scale reflect the following anchors and corresponding definitions:

"5" *Well defined yet permeable boundaries*: The ideal mixture of permeability and clarity of boundaries. There are no enmeshed behaviors that hinder good structure, conflict resolution, or task accomplishment; there are at least several differentiated responses.

"4" *Moderately well defined and/or moderately permeable boundaries*: Good, functional, but less than ideal boundaries. No mediated responses, mind readings, or global responses. Probably there are at least a few differentiated responses, although this is not critical. The majority of the other resonance variables are appropriate rather than inappropriate; that is, those behaviors are scarcely evidenced and their cumulative impact does not seriously disrupt family structure, task accomplishment, or conflict resolution.

"3" *Somewhat defined and/or somewhat permeable boundaries*: Although clear problems exist, boundaries are fairly functional. A limited number of mind readings, mediated responses, and undifferentiated responses may occur, but if they do, they are balanced by a few differentiated responses. Or, the other forms of resonance problems occur sometimes, and although they are often not severely impairing, their cumulative impact does tend to seriously disrupt family structure, task accomplishment, or conflict resolution. Or, boundaries seem generally acceptable but appropriate affective expression among members is missing.

"2" *Poorly defined or only slightly permeable boundaries*: Inappropriate boundaries are linked with other family dysfunction. The family is generally either enmeshed or disengaged. A few mediated responses, mind readings, or undifferentiated responses, *not* balanced by differentiated responses; or many mediated responses, mind readings, or undifferentiated responses balanced by only a few differentiated responses; or the other forms of resonance problems occur frequently.

"1"   *Nonexistent or impermeable boundaries*: Inappropriate boundaries are seriously jeopardizing family functioning. The family is either highly enmeshed or extremely disengaged. There are very few, if any, differentiated responses and many mediated responses, mind readings, and undifferentiated responses; other forms of resonance problems almost always occur.

Developmental Stage

The developmental stage scale is primarily a measure of the appropriateness of family members' interactions in terms of age, role, and tasks in their important family subsystems. These four sets of concerns are referred to as the parenting tasks and roles, spousal tasks and roles, sibling tasks and roles, and extended family tasks and roles, respectively. If the household includes extended family members (e.g., grandparents, aunts, uncles, etc.), then the functioning of these members must also be considered. Careful judgment is needed in ascertaining the appropriateness of interactions, especially with regard to the children. In making this judgment the rater should take into account the family's cultural heritage.

The following sets of roles and tasks are evaluated:

TABLE 3.4 Variables

Developmental Stage
1. Parenting roles and tasks
2. Spousal roles and tasks
3. Child/sibling roles and tasks
4. Extended family members' roles and tasks (if applicable)

Each inappropriate or inadequate performance at a role or task is scored under its appropriate subheading in the SFSR form. Then each of the four family tasks and roles categories are given an overall rating. This scale is rated on Tasks I, II, and III. The anchors for the developmental scale are presented below:

"5"   *Excellent developmental performance*: No flaws in the family's performance of tasks and roles. All sets of roles and tasks (parenting, spousal, sibling, and extended if applicable) function at an acceptable level relative to age and appropriately for their position in the family.

"4" *Good developmental performance*: All sets of roles and tasks generally function at an acceptable level relative to age and their position in the family, but there is at least one dysfunctional incident. The family is performing well at its tasks and roles, but with certain minor flaws. For example, a child may be treated a little too babyish for his age or, vice versa, be given some responsibilities beyond his age level.

"3" *Somewhat attenuated developmental performance*: One of the sets of roles and tasks functions inappropriately.

"2" *Maladaptive developmental performance*: Two of the sets of roles and tasks function inappropriately.

"1" *Very maladaptive developmental performance*: All sets of roles and tasks function inappropriately.

Identified Patienthood

This scale measures the extent to which the family considers the IP and his or her identified problem to be the sole problem of the family and uses that IPhood as a means of maintaining family homeostasis. There are five symptoms indicative of strong IPhood:

TABLE 3.5 Variables

Identified Patienthood
1. Negativity about the IP
2. IP centrality
3. Overprotection of the IPhood
4. Nurturance of IPhood
5. Denial of other problems

Another symptom serving to moderate IPhood is referred to as *Other Iphood*. While not necessarily a symptom of flexibility or good family development, Other IPhood does indicate that the family is capable of recognizing other problems rather than focusing solely on the IP and the presenting complaint. This moderating variable is extremely important in ascertaining the level of family functioning along this dimension.

Ratings are based on Tasks I and III only, using the following scoring guidelines:

"5" *Very flexible IPhood*: None of the five symptoms of strong IPhood are present. The moderating symptom (Other IPhood) may or may not be present.

"4" *Moderately flexible IPhood*: One and only one of the five symptoms of strong IPhood is present. The moderating symptom (Other IPhood) may or may not be present.

"3" *Somewhat flexible IPhood*: Two, three, or four of the five symptoms of strong IPhood are present, and the moderating symptom (Other IPhood) *is also* clearly present.

"2" *Moderately rigid IPhood*: *Two or three* of the five symptoms of strong IPhood are present, but the moderating symptom (Other IPhood) *is not* present. Or, *all five* symptoms of strong IPhood are present and the moderating symptom (Other IPhood) *is also* clearly present.

"1" *Very rigid IPhood*: *Four or all* of the five symptoms of strong IPhood are present, but the moderating symptom (Other IPhood) *is not* present.

Conflict Resolution

This scale is a measure of the family's ability to express, confront, and negotiate differences of opinion, disagreements, and conflict. It is important to observe and record the handling of differences and disagreements throughout all three tasks. Each family member's response (or lack of) to each task is also given a conflict resolution rating, given that each task is designed to elicit conflict. Each set of disagreements is placed into one of five categories:

TABLE 3.6 Variables

Conflict Resolution
1. Denial
2. Avoidance
3. Diffusion
4. Emergence without resolution
5. Emergence with resolution

In order to score the conflict resolution scale, *each and every difference and disagreement in Tasks I and II should be classified into one of the five categories.* After all the conflicts have been classified, a weighted average is calculated using the following weights: denial = 0, avoidance = 1, diffusion = 2, emergence without resolution = 3, and emergence with resolution = 5. Thus, for example, if a family had a total of

10 conflicts with 2 classified as denial, 4 classified as avoidance, 1 as diffusion, 2 as emergence without resolution, and 1 as emergence with resolution, the weighted average would be:

$$
\begin{aligned}
2 \times 0 &= 0 \\
4 \times 1 &= 4 \\
1 \times 2 &= 2 \\
2 \times 3 &= 6 \\
1 \times 5 &= \underline{5} \\
&\ 17 \qquad 17/10 = 1.70
\end{aligned}
$$

Ratings are then based on the following scoring criteria:

"5" *Excellent handling of conflicts*: Weighted average greater than or equal to 4.5. Most conflicts tend to emerge and at least some are adequately resolved.

"4" *Good handling of conflicts*: Weighted average greater than 3.5 and less than 4.5. Conflicts tend to emerge, although most are not resolved.

"3" *Moderate handling of conflicts*: Weighted average greater than 2.5 and equal to or less than 3.5. Most conflicts diffused, some avoided, and some emerged.

"2" *Poor handling of conflicts*: Weighted average greater than 1.5 and equal to or less than 2.5. Most conflicts denied, avoided, or diffused.

"1" *Very poor handling of conflicts*: Weighted average less than or equal to 1.5. Most conflicts denied or avoided. There is insignificant (if any) emergence.

II. ASSESSMENT AND DIAGNOSIS FOR USE IN CLINICAL PRACTICE

There are two ways of conducting a less than formal assessment when the information is only to be used clinically. The first of these, which we call the semiformal approach, is the one we most highly recommend for the initial assessment and diagnosis. The second, which we refer to as the informal approach, is integral to the ongoing process of therapy by which the therapist continuously reevaluates the family's functioning. Both of these approaches are complementary for clinical work, the semiformal approach being critical to the initial diagnosis and the informal approach being critical to the ongoing diagnostic process.

Semiformal Approach

This approach involves administering the Family Tasks as outlined earlier in this chapter. There are number of important advantages to the use of the Family Tasks for the initial assessment and diagnosis. First, families feel positive about undergoing a "standardized testing" procedure when they first come to see the therapist. In our experience, families perceived these tests as a sign that the therapist was thorough, caring, and had her or his "act together." Second, the therapist is able to derive cleaner, less confusing conclusions about the nature of family interactions when families are always responding to the same set of standardized interactions. By using a standard set of stimuli, it is easier to distinguish what about a response is elicited by the stimuli and what is unique to the individual/family. If we used, for example, a different set of words to determine vocabulary levels of different individuals, it would be difficult to compare the vocabulary capabilities across individuals. Similarly, if we attempt to assess the meaning of naturalistic interactions, letting the family determine the stimuli, it becomes more difficult, if not tricky, to determine how to compare families with each other. On the other hand, if we expose all families to standard stimuli, it is clear that once we learn the norms (which we have provided in Section I of this chapter in the form of Likert ratings), it is relatively straightforward to establish how a particular family's patterns of interactions are organized and how pathological they may be.

On the basis of the family's response to the Family Tasks, the therapist identifies "clinically" the family's maladaptation along the six dimensions, without formally conducting the SFSR. In our experience, *this is indeed a highly successful procedure.* Although not as fully reliable as the more formal scoring approach described above, it does provide the therapist with all the information needed to diagnose the family's maladaptive, repetitive patterns of behaviors at the time of the initial interview with the entire family.

The clinician would be well advised, however, to make several formal assessments with the SFSR as training in what to clinically look for. However, in our experience, once a therapist is well trained in the use of the SFSR, formal scoring is rarely if ever needed for clinical use. As we noted earlier, our preferred way of conducting a clinical assessment is to administer the Family Tasks in the formal way, including audiotaped instructions and videotaped responses. Then we either observe the family through the one-way mirror, or we review the videotape later.

Whereas the semiformal approach is a useful method for making a rapid and accurate assessment of the conjoint family at the initiation of therapy, BSFT also requires an ongoing process of assessment and diagnosis to guide the therapist with respect to the impact structural interventions may have had on the family, as well as to guide further interventions. The ongoing process of assessment and diagnosis is achieved through what we call the informal method. This method must be used without the formal trappings represented by the Family Tasks and the SFSR in order to avoid disrupting the ongoing therapeutic process.

Informal Approach

This approach to assessment and diagnosis is accomplished by eliciting enactments in which the clinician assists the family to behave in the therapy session as it usually would at home. Enactments are frequently elicited by assigning tasks that are relevant to the family process and moment (in contrast to the standardized Family Tasks). *Enactment* refers to encouraging or helping the family to behave/interact in its characteristic fashion, that is, as the family would naturally behave if the therapist were not present. To do this, the therapist systematically redirects communications to encourage interaction between family members rather than family–therapist interactions. In this fashion the therapist is able to elicit the family's natural way of operating and to make inferences about the family's functioning.

Typically, when the family comes to therapy, family members want to report their complaints and concerns. To allow them to report is useful as a strategy for establishing rapport because it is something they expect of the therapist (to listen) and because the therapist is then able to communicate concern and empathy (joining strategies as well). However, family members' reports may not be very useful in terms of providing the interactional or process information that the structural therapist requires. Thus the therapist wants to redirect communications targeted at the therapist to family–family interactions. It is only by observing directly the kinds of interactions that typically and repetitively occur in the family that the therapist can derive an accurate diagnosis.

The semiformal approach is highly recommended for the initial stage of therapy as a method for assessing family functioning, a less intrusive procedure such as the informal approach is required for repetitive administration throughout the therapeutic process. Whereas formal and semiformal assessments at the initial stage of therapy allows for the development of a treatment plan, analogous to charting an overall navigation plan for an entire boat trip, the informal approach to assessment is necessary for making the moment-to-moment adjustments needed to stay on course.

The informal approach, as noted, involves eliciting an enactment of the family's usual interactive patterns. For example, the mother says to the therapist, "Johnny is a mess." The therapist responds, "Would you say that to Johnny?" in an effort to elicit the kind of interaction that may occur at home when mother tells Johnny that he is a mess. The purpose of enactment is to encourage the family to interact in its usual way so that the therapist can observe the behavior patterns and identify, along the six interactional dimensions, which of them may be maladaptive.

This approach of encouraging enactment is not without its difficulties. For one, it erodes some of the therapist–family rapport, thus requiring extra effort in building rapport. Moreover, it requires considerable skill to prevent it from becoming a source of power struggles between family and therapist. Usually the mother will respond to the therapist's directive with "I tell Johnny all the time that he is a mess. What is the use of telling him again? What difference will it make?" Then the therapist explains that she or he wants to observe what happens, and the mother, somewhat irritated and with great hesitancy, complies.

There are thus three ways of conducting the assessment and diagnosis of the family. The most formal and rigorous procedure, recommended for research and evaluation purposes, is the administration of both the Family Tasks and the SFSR. The assessment is conducted by collecting information through the Family Tasks—the standard stimuli. The diagnosis is conducted by formally scoring and/or interpreting these data along the six structural dimensions, using the SFSR.

The semiformal approach is recommended for therapists who wish to obtain rapid and accurate clinical information for their initial diagnosis. This approach involves the formal administration of the Family Tasks only. The interpretation of the information provided by the Family Tasks is then done "clinically," based on the general guidelines established in the SFSR, although the latter is *not* formally used for scoring.

The informal approach is used in making the ongoing assessment of family functioning needed to guide the therapists in making moment-to-moment adjustments, in order to increase the likelihood of successfully achieving the goals of the treatment plan. In this case, the therapist elicits the family's usual interactive patterns during therapy and uses this information to adjust the course of therapy and update the diagnosis as needed.

4

Diagnosis: What Works Well and What Needs to Be Fixed

The strategic character of BSFT emerges clearly during diagnosis. This is because our diagnoses are not intended to feed academic curiosity about theoretical formulations. They are made solely to identify adaptive and maladaptive interactions (structures) so that *strategically efficient* interventions can be *planned* to bring about desired change.

This chapter illustrates the use of the semiformal approach to assessment and diagnosis described in the last chapter. This chapter is addressed to clinicians or family therapists who wish to apply the basic concepts inherent in the SFSR to their clinical practice, without being burdened by the formal trappings necessary for elegant diagnostic procedures.

DIAGNOSIS IN CLINICAL PRACTICE

In defining what works well and what needs to be fixed, we must invariably choose reference standards, which are invariably arbitrary—at least, more or less. In a problem-focused strategic approach like the one proposed here, it is wise to limit the scope of what needs to be fixed to "If it isn't broken, don't fix it." That is, in therapies oriented toward resolving a particular set of presenting problems, unless a particular interactional pattern is directly related to the existence of a symptom, we recommend not fixing it.

Needless to say, this is not a hard-and-fast rule. Something may not be "broken," and yet it may not "work well" either. If an interaction pattern is maladaptive because it permits or at least is unable to stop the existence of a symptom (that is, "it is broken") and we fix it (that is, we correct it), then we call this *treatment*. However, there are many instances in which we observe an interactive pattern that appears to be maladaptive but has not yet produced a symptom. In these cases, it is a judgment call whether or not we should attempt to fix it and thus *prevent* the emergence or occurrence of a possible or probable symptom. Whether or not we attempt to carry out preventive interventions usually depends on the extensiveness and severity of problems that have brought the family to our attention. It is most strategic (in the sense that it works best) to treat first the symptoms brought to us. Unless we meet the family's expectations in this regard, the family is unlikely to stay around long enough for us to either treat or prevent. Thus, if we think in terms of a risk-benefit analysis, we are less likely to lose the family if we first treat the family's complaints, meeting the family's expectations of symptom relief, and then move to preventive interventions if the family is willing to give us the time. The alternative (attempting the preventive interventions first) comes with a greater risk, since these interventions violate the family's expectations and thus increase the risk that the family will leave therapy before we ever get to intervene and correct the more urgent problems that brought the family to us.

While throughout much of this book the emphasis is on providing examples of cases where there are symptoms, it may be worthwhile here to illustrate some examples of a structural diagnosis of a family that uses high-risk interactive patterns but in which serious symptoms have not yet emerged. In the example presented below, the Albertini family was administered the Family Tasks. The Albertini family consists of mother, father, a 12-year-old son, and a 14-year-old daughter. The results obtained from the Family Tasks were used to determine the family's functioning along the six structural dimensions:

1. *Structure*: Mother–child alliance; father peripheral. Children's communication mostly through mother.
2. *Flexibility*: Around child-rearing issues mother is responsible nearly all the time. Around other topics, such as making a menu, mother and father ally occasionally.
3. *Resonance*: Mother indicates what son prefers to eat, and mother and son laugh together, both signs of enmeshment. Father is

frequently "too busy" to participate in family activities, a sign of disengagement. Complaints about each other during Family Tasks are highly specific, a sign of adaptive functioning along this dimension.

4. *Developmental stage*: Children are not allowed to play outdoors at night. Mother shares with son complaints about father coming home late.

5. *Identified patienthood*: Father comes home late; does not help with chores at home. Son is rebellious and had conduct problems in school. Daughter is "model child."

6. *Conflict resolution*: Conflicts either emerge without resolution or are diffused.

In the Albertini family the parents have allocated to themselves separate role responsibilities, with the mother fully responsible for all child rearing and the father's responsibility in this regard being highly limited (either because mother prefers it that way, father prefers it that way, or, as occurs in the vast majority of cases, both parents, each for their own reason, prefer it that way). Hence we have identified a maladaptive structure in that around child-rearing issues father and mother are not allied with each other. Rather, it may appear that mother and son are the ones allied around these issues and that father is peripheral. If we look a little further, we would not be surprised to find that the same structure occurred around content areas other than child rearing. In fact, these kinds of interactive patterns or structures are typically found to be quite pervasive and, if found to occur around one content, are almost invariably occurring around some, if not all, contents.

We started by presenting this family as not yet having a severe symptom around this structural problem and thus suggest that intervention in this interactive pattern at this time may be construed as preventive. If the interactive pattern is identical to that found in a family with a severe symptom, why does this family not yet have a severe symptom? Probably because this family has not yet been challenged by the severe stresses that accompany the developmental milestone of a child's moving into adolescence. When this child or young adolescent begins to shift more fully into the adolescent years (during which the child, like a tropical storm moving over warm Caribbean waters, begins to pick up strength and can turn into a hurricane), the family will be completely unable to set limits to the youth's behavior. At that time the lack of a strong parental alliance around child-rearing issues will totally undermine the family's ability to chart an effective and successful course of action, and the youngster will develop one or more symptoms that, as discussed in Chapter 1, we usually label the behavior problem syndrome, which since the 1970s has typically included drug abuse.

Like in the analogy of the tropical depression or storm moving over the warm Caribbean waters and acquiring its strength from the warmth of the waters, forces external to the family contribute to the emergence of the behavior problem syndrome, such as peer group influences and the norms that exist or to which the youth is exposed outside the home. These extrafamilial forces provide the impetus for the rebellion. The likelihood of their occurrence is part of what determines the level of risk. What is certain, however, is that if they do occur, and if the family attempts to meet this challenge with the kind of inadequate or maladaptive structure described earlier, the family will fail. The result will be a group of related acting-out behaviors on the part of the child.

There are some social scientists who work at changing the peer norms, and this is clearly an adaptive macro-intervention. The approach recommended here is more limited in scope, easier to implement, and undoubtedly more clinical in nature. This approach involves changing the interactive pattern in the family that, in this case, is preventing the family from successfully charting the youth's path—or in other words, from successfully providing parental leadership to the youth. Our approach, then, restores parents' leadership capabilities within the family. This is based on the belief or value that it is important as well as useful to promote parents' capability to be strong, successful family leaders.

Returning to the earlier description of the problem with the Albertini family, when we first see the case prior to the emergence of serious problems, we may observe at that time potential difficulties along some of the other family interactional dimensions. As noted in Chapter 2, the structural dimension is the central dimension that defines interactive difficulties; when structural maladaptations exist, they give rise to a whole host of maladaptations in the other dimensions. Thus, for example, when we observe a structure in which father is left out (or chooses to remain outside) of child-rearing decisions, and we suggest that this interactive pattern is probably reflective of what typically occurs on most topics, not just child rearing, we are implicitly suggesting that this is an inflexible family. Lack of flexibility is defined when the family tends to interact in the same way regardless of the appropriateness or adaptiveness of that pattern of interactions. Thus we have determined that this is a family with moderately low flexibility. Clearly, if the family can change the way it interacts (i.e., the way it organizes itself) in response to different tasks or stressors or stimuli, then we would not be able to diagnose a repetitive maladaptive structure.

With respect to our third dimension of resonance, it becomes clear that if father is outside of the mother–child alliance, then father is less affected by what goes on within that alliance and, by the very fact of his being peripheral, is emotionally distant (disengaged). In comparison to father, mother and youth are much closer emotionally and psychologically, and thus they might run the risk of becoming enmeshed (if they are not already). Whether or not we define the mother–child dyad as enmeshed and/or the father as disengaged from the mother–child, it is obvious that there is a difference in the psychological and emotional distance that exists between father and mother and father and son on the one hand, and mother and son on the other.

Maladaptiveness in the three remaining family interactional dimensions, prior to the development of severe symptoms, may be more or less clear. At this early stage developmental level may reveal that in some respects the youth may not have been given yet enough liberties, whereas in others the son may be burdened with responsibilities that are more appropriately assigned to a spouse/father.

At this early stage it is unlikely that the IPhood is clearly lodged on the son. Rather, the IPhood in the Albertini family may be lodged in the father, as a "tool" for keeping father distant. Later on, when the son develops more severe symptoms, the IPhood might shift and become more clearly lodged in the youth.

With regard to conflict resolution, to the extent that father and mother are not making deicisions together, we may speculate that differences of opinion are not being resolved. We would expect that if father and mother agreed on how to rear their child, then, almost by definition, they would be allies. The fact that two people living in such close quarters are not allies makes us suspect that differences of opinions (i.e., conflicts) are not being resolved.

FROM ASSESSMENT TO DIAGNOSIS TO TREATMENT

Understanding the six dimensions that characterize family system functioning goes a long way toward assisting us in defining what we must do as therapists: We diagnose the problem in terms of these six areas and implement strategies to correct problems along these six areas (some more than others). Thus if we took as an example the Albertini family 5 years later, when the behavior problem syndrome is evident in the 17-year-old son, we might diagnose the problem in terms of (1) inadequate structure defined by ineffective behavior control, resulting from improper alliances; (2) maladaptive resonance in which one parent is too close (enmeshed) with one child whereas a second parent is too far (disengaged) from the spouse and that same child; (3) inappropriate developmental stage, with the enmeshed child having too little responsibility in some areas while being burdened by spousal roles in others; (4) rigid identification of the enmeshed child as the only family problem; (5) and, finally, repeated emergence of certain conflicts that never get resolved, perhaps in this case because they are avoided and/or become diffused. Now that problems have become more serious, the family's conflict resolution style has deteriorated since the earlier assessment.

Having diagnosed the problem in terms of these structural systems dimensions, it is possible to target interventions directly at these dimensions. For example, one of the first moves of the therapist will usually be to attack rigid IPhood by spreading the IPhood around. This is accomplished by identifying sources of pain other than those related to the child's behavior. The therapist may find (and highlight) that other family members are manifesting problems, or that everyone else is less than perfect, thereby modifying the rigid IPhoof and opening others to change. For example; "It looks like daughter comes home late, and you worry"; "Hmmm, when your husband goes fishing and leaves you alone with the problem, it must be very annoying to you"; "I didn't realize you had such a stressful position; no wonder sometimes when you become tense you want to be by yourself."

Next, the therapist may target structure and resonance by having the disengaged parent (i.e., father) get closer to the problem youth. Immediately following this initial intervention, a dialogue may be initiated between the two parents about this youth, with the purpose of beginning to establish an alliance between the parents around the content of their mutual concern for their son. A next step may be to encourage negotiation between the parents around the setting of rules for the child, which, one implemented, would bring under control unmanageable behavior. Finally, in the process of negotiation, conflict avoidance and then diffusion occur, and it becomes necessary for the therapist to direct the negotiations sufficiently to allow for a new set of skills to be practiced: conflict emergence and then resolution.

INTERRELATIONSHIP BETWEEN DIMENSIONS

As can be seen from the discussion above, it was never our intention to imply that the six structural dimensions are independent or, in the statistical sense, orthogonal. Rather, these dimensions occur in an *interdependent* fashion. Thus, for example, IPhood is a reflection of the inflexibility of the system. In a similar fashion inappropriate develop-

TABLE 4.1

Steps	How
Spread IPhood	By identifying sources of pain other than child/IP
Create new alliances: Father-child Father-mother	Give father-son a task together. Once father is closer to child, use father's and mother's focus on the child as the problem to encourage father and mother to work on some common solution to child's problem behavior.
Work on conflict resolution style	Conflict resolution style is enacted when parents attempt to set rules together. Therapist intervenes to facilitate emergence with resolution.
Maintain the gains reached above	Repeat processes outlined above as needed until it "sticks."

mental stage may also be a reflection of inflexibility in moving from one stage to another.

Frequently crossgenerational alliances represent simultaneously a problem in structure with a maladaptive alliance and a likely problem in resonance, with, for example, the child–mother dyad being too close (enmeshed) and the child–father dyad not close enough (disengaged).

Our six dimensions of family functioning are like the proverbial four blind men describing the elephant, each providing a true, but different, perspective. In the case of our six family-functioning dimensions, each provides a slightly different perspective of a single, albeit complex, family process.

It has been our hope to illustrate through the example of the Albertini family that diagnosis in terms of the structural systems dimensions is an extremely useful step in the treatment process because it directs the therapist immediately to maladaptive interactional patterns that are likely to result in unwanted behaviors or prevent the family from meeting its desired objectives.

It should now be clearer to the reader how it is possible to conduct BSFT in cases involving behavior problem and drug-abusing youths within our usual time limit of 12 sessions. One powerful reason for the brevity of the therapy is the preciseness of the intervention. Such preciseness is made possible by the simplicity and clarity of the nature of the problem to be resolved. One powerful reason it is so simple and clear is our diagnostic procedure. We believe that diagnostic procedure is sufficiently important to devote to it three full chapters in this book.

Part III

Treatment

The third section of this book presents the intervention approach known as Brief Strategic Family Therapy: a strategic, time-limited, problem-focused intervention model that capitalizes fully on systems and structural theories. From systems theory we obtain the notion of the interdependency of family members, and from structural theory we obtain the notion that the repetitive patterns of interactions among family members represent the critical unit for therapeutic study and intervention.

Chapter 5 reviews structural family therapy intervention strategies and their application to conjoint family therapy. A case example of BSFT in the conjoint mode is also presented. This review chapter provides the foundation for following chapters in which novel strategies are proposed, based on the fundamental concepts and strategies of BSFT.

5

Brief Strategic
Family Therapy

*William M. Kurtines, Olga Hervis,
and José Szapocznik*

The foundation for the concepts and strategies for treating the maladaptive patterns of interactions that we review in this chapter is rooted in
structural family theory and therapy. We have built on this foundation to
develop BSFT, as described in this chapter. This therapeutic model builds
solidly on the concepts of systems and structure while thoroughly inte-
grating the concepts of strategy, within the context of a time-limited
approach. We do not necessarily consider the combination of concepts
and strategies that comprise BSFT to be a major breakthrough in family
therapy—as compared to the major breakthroughs in assessment, diagnosis, engagement, and family therapy through one person, described else-
where in this book—but we feel that it makes a substantial contribution
to the advancement of family theory and therapy.

Consistent with its roots in structural systems family therapy, BSFT is present and future oriented. Its goal is not the exploration of the past but rather the manipulation of the present as a tool for change. In order to work toward this goal, the therapist looks at sets of family interactions, diagnoses those that are maladaptive, and plans strategies to change maladaptive interactional patterns using techniques referred to as restructuring.

A systems approach does not rely on linear causality, as is suggested when a current event is said to be caused by a past event. Rather, a systems approach is built on circular paths of causality in which current events are *inter*dependent among each other, so that, for example, the symptom and the maladaptive interactions "cause each other" and keep each other "alive." Figure 1.2 (p. 11) illustrates the concept of circular causality. Structural therapy works by interrupting the cycle of causality, changing those repetitive interactions that are interdependent with the undesirable symptom. Once these maladaptive interactions are replaced by more adaptive and flexible patterns, the symptom disappears.

This chapter introduces the basic therapeutic techniques used in BSFT and illustrates the application of these techniques with a case history. This introduction is brief and assumes that the reader already has background and experience in working with families.

STRUCTURAL FAMILY THERAPY TECHNIQUES

The major therapeutic techniques that BSFT uses fall into the three traditional structural family therapy categories: joining, diagnosis, and restructuring techniques (Minuchin, 1974). Although they can be discussed separately, these three sets of techniques are usually applied in an integrated fashion in therapy. Because diagnosis was extensively discussed in the three previous chapters, this chapter focuses on joining and restructuring.

Joining

While the goal of therapy is to bring about changes, bringing about change is a most challenging task. Structural therapists take advantage of their understanding of systems and their structure to enter the family system, minimizing the likelihood of resistance and rejection. It stands to reason that if our ultimate goal is to change the family's pattern of interactions, we must first place ourselves in a position vis-à-vis the family from which we will be permitted to bring about these changes. In our work we place as much, if not more, emphasis on the joining stage—

that is, the stage in which we position ourselves—than in the restructuring phase. In our experience, restructuring can be relatively easy when we are properly accepted by the family in a leadership role; conversely, restructuring can be a road filled with insurmountable obstacles when the family does not feel fully comfortable with us and decides to resist our efforts. It is for these reasons that we view the creation of a new therapeutic system an essential preamble to creating change within a family. In joining it is essential that the therapist accept the family organization as is, thus eliminating the possibility of perceiving an artificial system or of alienating the family. According to Minuchin (1974), there are three types of joining interventions:

1. Maintenance involves supporting the family structures. A family system is governed by rules that regulate the behavior of its members. The therapist joining the family feels the pressure to behave according to these rules. He or she may accept them in the beginning as a way of gaining entrance to the system. For example, if the mother is the central pathway by which family communication is routed, the therapist also talks to her and allows her to mediate his communications to the family. The therapist must be aware of the family's threshold of stress. When family members need support, the therapist will provide it. When change-producing strategies are pushing the family toward its threshold, the therapist will use maintenance techniques to move back to a point where the family is more comfortable. Other examples of maintenance operations are supporting areas of family strength, rewarding or affiliating with a family member, supporting an individual member who feels threatened by therapy, and explaining a problem.

In our experience with families with drug-abusing youths, it is usually important to support both the parents and the youth very early in the therapy by empathizing with the parents' pain and with the youth's annoyance at being brought to therapy. Both of these supportive interventions are examples of maintenance.

2. Tracking is a method of adopting the content of family communications or utilizing the nature of family interactions. There are two kinds of tracking: content and process tracking. As a phonograph follows a record's grooves, producing sound, the therapist takes over the family's content and process using them in therapeutic maneuvers. For example, a family may be complaining about the father's authoritarian stance. The father says, "I want to be a leader, but I want to be a democratic leader. I want to be the president of this family." The therapist says, "Okay, if you want to be a democratic leader, let's hold an election." In tracking, the therapist does not challenge the family. The patient is never confronted. The therapist asks the family what is the problem that brings them to therapy. The mother answers, and soon it becomes clear that the mother

is not only the most vocal person in the family but also that she is the gatekeeper who controls the flow of communications. When the therapist notices that the IP is not verbalizing what she/he feels, perceives, but rather, mother is speaking for the youth, the therapist asks the mother's permission to address the youth directly and explore what the youth's point of view may be: "Do you mind if I ask your son about this?" As in the technique of jujitsu, one uses the opponent's own movement to propel him. With a family, the therapist utilizes the family's movement to propel it. But he maintains the framework that he is propelling it in the direction in which it wants to go. He seems to enter the family as a supporter of family rules. But he makes the family rules work in the direction of his goals for it.

In order to facilitate tracking, the therapist encourages enactment of typical family interactional styles. As indicated earlier, enactment refers to helping the family to behave/interact in its characteristic fashion.

With drug-abusing youths, the youth is frequently the most powerful person in the family. As an example of process tracking, the therapist would ally with the youth in order to bring the family into treatment.

3. The third joining technique, mimesis, is aimed at the family's style and affect, as reflected in the member's activity and mood. The therapist may use the tempo of family communications. If the family is restricted, his communications may be sparse. He may adopt the family's affective style. In a jovial, expansive family, he may use expansive body movements. He pays attention to their language and begins to use some of their terms. If they discuss a bar mitzvah, he may use a Yiddish word. If a Puerto Rican family is urging a daughter to find a husband, he may suggest that she turn St. Anthony's statue upside down. Mimetic operations are mostly nonexplicit and quite spontaneous. Experienced therapists perform them without realizing it. In one family, a father who was derogating himself took his coat off. Immediately, the therapist took his own coat off. (Minuchin, 1974, p. 184)

Restructuring

Once a therapeutic system is established, and once the family has been permitted to operate in its usual fashion, the conditions have now been established for the family to feel accepted by the therapist and to accept and admit the therapist into its midst—to permit the therapist to assume a leadership role. As such the therapist can now undertake to bring about changes in the family's patterns of interaction by promoting, facilitating, suggesting, and actually directing alternate organizations, structural arrangements, and interactional patterns. The therapist challenges the family's status quo, tests its flexibility in response to change, and creates situations that permit more adaptive alternatives to emerge. These change-producing interventions aimed at changing the family's structure (i.e., patterns of interactions) are referred to as restructuring. There are a variety of ways in which change-producing interventions can be made. Some of these techniques enable the therapist to change the family's repetitive patterns of interaction by shifting alliances or changing boundaries within the family system. For example, maladaptive patterns of interaction can be blocked by the therapist while new interactions are prescribed. In this work the therapist uses space creatively, changing the physical and emotional position of family members or using himself/herself to encourage certain communications and block others.

Because restructuring interventions are usually stressful, they may erode some of the goodwill that the therapist created during the earlier joining maneuvers. For this reason, while restructuring it is important to continue joining activities. In particular, the therapist needs to apply maintenance techniques in order to prevent the family from being overly stressed. Thus even though it is sometimes necessary to create a stressful crisis situation, oftentimes the therapist applies maintenance techniques to keep the stress within a tolerable range and to maintain the family engaged and in treatment.

A number of techniques can be used to restructure and shift family interactional patterns:

Reframing

The therapist relabels a process, a person, or an event, creating a new reality for the family. An alternative understanding is proposed that implies a new way of behaving. A classic example of reframing, although not within a family context, was President Ronald Reagan's renaming of the MX missile as the Peacekeeper, thereby attempting to deflect the criticism of pro-peace advocates. An example in family therapy is found in the case of a father who berated his son for drug use and school failures. The son felt rejected by the father and thus responded with anger toward him. The therapist wanted to change the interaction in order to build a bridge of communication. This was achieved when the therapist created a new sense of reality about this interaction by reframing the interaction, saying to the father in the presence of the son, "I can see that you are deeply concerned about your son and worried about his future." The father's anger quickly melted, and he spoke about his concern and care. The son no longer felt rejected. Rather, he felt the father's caring.

Reversals

The therapist changes a habitual pattern of interacting by coaching one member of the family to say or do the opposite of her of his usual response. A reversal of the established sequence breaks up previously rigid pathological patterns and allows new alternatives to emerge. A rather somber fellow who always gets angry when his wife nags him to be joyful and smiley is taught by the therapist to respond with a genuine "I am not smiling because this is how I am." Another example occurs within the same family when the father gets angry for having been nagged and yells at his 16-year-old conduct problem daughter. In response, father and daughter begin to fight. A reversal in this case would entail having the daughter respond differently to her father by saying "Daddy, I love you when you get angry like that" or "Daddy, I get very frightened when you get angry like that."

Detriangulation

Triangles were defined in an earlier chapter in terms of a third, usually less powerful, person being involved in a conflict between two others. The only way for a dyad to resolve conflict is dyadically. Bringing in a third person and forming a triangle becomes an obstacle to conflict resolution. Since triangulation prevents dyadic relationships from processing and growth, the goal of therapy is to break the triangle. Detriangulation permits the dyad in conflict to transact "business" or feelings directly and thus more effectively. Detriangulation also frees the third party from being used as the repository of the system's problems (i.e., becoming an IP). For example, in a family where there is an alliance between mother and son, as well as a marital conflict, the father frequently gets at the mother by denigrating and belittling the son. It may be that the son and the mother actually pair up to keep the father distant from the family. When the father wants to get to the mother, he can do so by placing his son in an IP role. Detriangulation of the son may be achieved by breaking up the alliance between the mother and son. This may be done by having the son participate with the father in activities, such as sports.[1] Actual detriangulation can now be accomplished by coaching the son to set boundaries between himself and the parental couple, particularly when conflict emerges between the parents. This can be accomplished by having the son leave the scene of an argument. Thus, now when the father wants to get to the mother, the son won't stay around to act as a repository of the conflict's blame. Hence father and mother are forced to address the conflict more directly.

Opening Up Closed Systems

Families in which the conflicts are not overt need help in bringing the conflict to the surface so that it is accessible for therapeutic work. One way to make conflicts overt and realistically confront the root of the problem, is to activate the conflict by magnifying small emotional

---

[1]This could also be construed as a reversal of the father–son relationship.

issues, thereby creating crises. This in turn activates dormant interactions so that they can be dealt with openly and in a new manner. A classic example is the spouse who feels oppressed and depressed but is unable to respond to the oppressing spouse, such as the case of the meek husband who is constantly nagged by his wife, or the case of the overbearing husband with a depressed, martyred wife. The therapist may work with oppressed spouses to help them clarify for their own selves what their feelings are and, subsequently, support and encourage the oppressed spouse to express these feelings to the other spouse, and perhaps to state his/her desire and/or demands for change. In working with families with drug-abusing adolescents, a typical example occurs in the case of peripheral fathers who tend to deny or avoid any discussion of the youth's problems. In one somewhat controversial case familiar to the authors, a youth who was stealing was advised by the therapist to begin to steal from his parents. The father quickly became involved in the case.

Homework Tasks

The new interactions fostered in therapy sessions by these techniques are strengthened by the assignment of tasks. An essential aspect of BSFT is that in order to promote generalization of the new patterns emerging during therapy, the family is given a task (homework) at each session that repeats, in the natural context, the in-therapy experience. Thus various family members are directed to carry out certain interactions at home, after the interactions have been successfully carried out in a therapy session. The task must consist of interactions between persons rather than something one person can do on her or his own.

WALKING THROUGH THE CASE OF THE HERNANDEZ FAMILY

The Hernandez family sought treatment on the recommendation of the school counselor because of concerns over the Hernandez' 16-year-old daughter, Sussy. Sussy's Aunt Rosa made the initial contact with the Center, seeking professional help. Aunt Rosa told the therapist that she, as well as Pedro and Susana, Sussy's parents, had become concerned about her truancy and possible drug abuse.

DIAGNOSTIC INTERVIEW

The first step in the case of the Hernandez family was the initial interview and diagnostic session. For the interview Sussy was dressed in a private school uniform and gave an impression of being an innocent young woman. As the Hernandez family entered the office and seated themselves, Aunt Rosa sat nearest the therapist, with Susana (Mrs. Hernandez) next, then Sussy, and finally, Pedro (Mr. Hernandez).

TABLE 5.1 Seating Arrangement for Diagnostic Interview

	+ Susana	
+ Rosa		+ Sussy
* Therapist		
	+ Pedro	

All four sat in a way that kept Pedro out of the interaction. Family seating patterns are often important clues to more general structural patterns. In this case Pedro's isolation was immediately evident from the seating pattern.

Aunt Rosa, while very conservative and traditionally Cuban in her outlook on life, appeared a strong and determined woman. She quickly took charge of the session, presenting the family to the therapist and unhesitatingly expressing detailed negative accounts and multiple complaints about Sussy. She presented her complaints in a dramatic and animated fashion, which added to the emotionally charged atmosphere of the interview. Rosa's list of complaints about Sussy included (1) frequent truancy, (2) drug use (marijuana, Quaaludes), (3) poor academic grades, and (4) disobedience and disrespect. Aunt Rosa said she found all these things out from the school counselor, as well as from letters that she had discovered in Sussy's desk. As the interview progressed, Sussy frequently interrupted Aunt Rosa and her parents, denying everything. She claimed that the problem was that they would not leave her alone, that they had it in for her friends, who were the only ones who really understood her. The initial interview thus took place in an atmosphere of an emotional uproar marked by accusations and weeping. The atmosphere of the interview, overcharged by the agitated voices of the three women, contrasted with Pedro's depressed and apathetic voice.

In formulating a diagnosis it is important to examine the family as a whole, in terms of interactions and interrelationships. The therapist avoids casting family members into polarly opposed roles, providing instead a systemic understanding of the interactions, recognizing that every member of the family contributes toward maintaining the system. It is assumed therefore that all family members contribute to and have an investment in maintaining the systemic status quo.

The Hernandez family was administered the Family Tasks. The information provided by the Family Tasks was not formally scored using the SFSR but rather was used as the basis for a semiformal clinical assessment and diagnosis, with the following results.

Structure

Communication Flow

Rosa functioned as the spokesperson and gatekeeper of the family. There was a lack of directness in Sussy's communication with her father because of Rosa's interferences.

Subsystem Organization

Rosa and Sussy functioned as a parent–child subsystem that was highly conflictual. Susana, Sussy's mother, allied with Rosa and supported her in a parental role, while Pedro, Sussy's father, was peripheral. Leadership was in the hands of Rosa rather than in the hands of the parents. Leadership was shared at times between Rosa and Susana.

Flexibility

Subsystem formation was persistent, although alliances shifted between Rosa and Sussy, and Rosa and Susana. Pedro always remained peripheral.

Resonance

Rosa and Sussy were enmeshed, while Pedro was disengaged. Differentiation is relatively specific, in the sense that family members were able to make precise complaints about each other.

Developmental Stage

Sussy was treated as a 12-year-old and did not have the independence of a teenager her age. Similarly, she did not fully accept responsibilities for a youth her age. Extended family members had far too much responsibility.

Identified Patienthood

While Sussy was identified as the primary culprit of the family's suffering, Pedro was a secondary IP in this family. Pedro and Susana felt like failures as parents.

Conflict Resolution

Conflict diffusion was the most prevalent conflict resolution style, although occasionally some conflicts were avoided, and others were discussed but not resolved.

Structurally, then, the family's diagnosis suggests that Aunt Rosa functioned in a parental role with the direct support of Susana. A highly enmeshed and conflictual relationship existed between Rosa and Sussy. Pedro was alienated from the family. When an effort was made to have Susana and Pedro discuss parenting issues and differences that arose, Aunt Rosa quickly sided with Susana. The two of them easily over-powered Pedro, who retreated to his passive, depressed, and withdrawn peripheral family role.

Aunt Rosa, an extended family member, was overly involved and functioned inappropriately in a parental role. Pedro and Susana felt like failures as parents. At the age of 66 Pedro felt excessively tired and was unable to understand what had happened to his little girl, much less to exercise control over her. Susana, at 55, with a factory job and house-work duties, insisted that it was Pedro, already retired, who should keep a close watch over Sussy and her acquaintances. Aunt Rosa quickly took Susana's side, badgered Pedro for not being "a man and a father," and moved into the power vacuum left by Susana and Pedro's inability to parent. Thus the parental subsystem had totally abdicated its power and executive function. Sussy, on the other hand, by using her IPhood and rejecting her parents as too old and too traditionally Cuban, had gained considerable power, which she used to manipulate both her parents and Aunt Rosa.

The patterns of interaction that characterized the Hernandez family can be visually depicted through a structural map. In structural family therapy, mapping is frequently used in understanding the family as a structural system. In our own work the structural map is a particularly useful adjunct to assessment and diagnosis because it helps to depict visually the dimensions of structure, resonance, and IPhood. Figure 5.1A is a map of the Hernandez family as revealed through the Family Task in which Aunt Rosa (A), the major power figure, exerted power over a rebellious Sussy (D) and, to a lesser extent, over Susana (M) and Pedro (F). Pedro was isolated. Figure 5.1B is a map of the desired goal of therapy, in which Pedro and Susana exercise successful leadership in the family, with Aunt Rosa sharing in the leadership through a more supportive role.

Joining

The therapist begins the joining process by attempting to form a therapeutic alliance. In BSFT it is important during the joining phase to attempt to establish an alliance with the entire family (by respecting and supporting the family process) as well as with each of its members (by allying with each family member's agenda). The joining process is

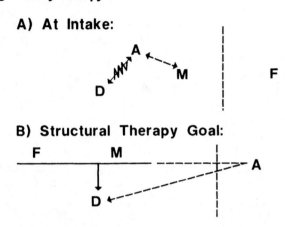

FIGURE 5.1 Map of the Hernandez family system.

an essential foundation for other work and, indeed, must continue throughout therapy. It is critical therefore to join effectively in order to allow the therapist to progress to restructuring.

The therapist joins by encouraging the family to enact its typical style of interacting and then initially supporting the family's interactional style. It should be noted that in cases where family interactions are less dramatic or dynamic, it is sometimes necessary for the therapist to take a more active role in eliciting family enactments. This can often be done by establishing a temporary alliance with one of the family members and then using that alliance to provoke a minor crisis. Under conditions of minor crises families often display interactional patterns that might not emerge during the course of the therapy sessions. This procedure is what we referred to earlier as opening up a closed system.

Throughout the joining process, the therapist joins each family member by talking with her or him individually (but with the whole family present) in an empathic way. That is, the therapist must convince each individual that she or he is accepted and understood by the therapist. Each individual must experience an alliance with the therapist, but, in fact, the therapist must maintain an ability to establish alliances with all family members as needed, as well as an ability to "move out" of the system and, on occasion, remain detached, objective, and nonjudgmental. Thus, for example, the therapist joined Aunt Rosa by saying that it was well known that she had given Sussy a lot of love and care—an example of maintenance. With Sussy, the therapist attended to what she said with respect and dignity, in contrast to the adults in her family who treated her both like a monster and a baby.

With the parents the therapist used mimesis by exchanging baby pictures with Susana and quoting famous sayings to Pedro, who often used them himself. Note that by talking to Sussy as an adult and by sharing baby pictures with Susana, the therapist was symbolically reframing by clarifying that Sussy was no longer a baby and must not be treated as one. With this approach, as in most cases of "good therapy," the therapist must always behave in a manner with which she or he is comfortable and that is appropriate to the circumstances. For example, this particular therapist was a woman about 30 years of age, much younger than the other adults present. Therefore even though she had to establish herself as an expert and a leader, she had to guard against appearing disrespectful toward the older adults. If the therapist had been older, a different approach to joining might have been more useful for that therapist. The joining process, therefore, must be adapted to the style of the therapist and the client.

During the joining process the therapist discovered that Aunt Rosa was a childless widow whose life had become dedicated to the family. Her house was a block away from that of the Hernandez family. On her visits to the family, which were quite frequent, she came on foot since her doctor had prohibited her from driving. Because Rosa was such an energetic woman, she had assumed many parenting responsibilities that Pedro, using age as his excuse, and Susana, using work as hers, had been unable and/or unwilling to assume. It was during the joining and through the opportunity to enact typical interactional styles that Aunt Rosa's sense of responsibility and traditional conservatism, but also her great energy, had become evident and appeared to complement Sussy's growing adolescent search for identity and exuberant sense of independence. Both Rosa's and Sussy's styles contrasted with the relatively passive roles that Pedro and Susana appeared to have taken within the family.

In summary, the joining should (1) give the therapist an opportunity to accept each family member and the family system as a whole, (2) allow the therapist to be accepted by the family, (3) establish the therapist as an expert leader, and (4) allow the therapist to observe and confirm the diagnosis of the repetitive sequences and styles of interactions that characterize the family.

Restructuring

BSFT is built on certain beliefs and values about what is adaptive in terms of family structure. Thus, for example, we believe that parents, whenever feasible, have to be in the leadership role in the nuclear family, with extended family members cast in supportive roles. We also believe that whenever a parent is disengaged from nuclear family operations, there is an increased likelihood for acting out or uncontrolled behavior—including drug use—on the part of a youth. This is the case because the youth is able to play on the split parental authority. In the case of the Hernandez family it was clear that power in the family had to be redistributed. Aunt Rosa and Sussy had taken over control of the family, Aunt Rosa by virtue of her forceful personality and Sussy by virtue of her IPhood. Pedro and Susana had become passive observers in the family and needed to regain control. As soon as this maladaptive pattern became clear, the therapist temporarily assumed the executive function of the family and, as discussed below, began to guide the parents toward taking on these executive functions themselves. The therapist had to assume it first, in order to remove Aunt Rosa from that role so that Pedro and Susana would experience less resistance to filling the resulting "power gap." As would typically occur, the restructuring was complicated by the fact that everyone in the family was receiving secondary gains from the current structural arrangement. Pedro continued to be preoccupied by his age, and the fact that he was always "too tired" meant that he didn't have to be bothered by Sussy's need for attention. Susana could continue to use her job and housework as an excuse for not taking responsibility for rearing Sussy. Aunt Rosa clearly benefited by playing a central role in the family, and Sussy was the center of attention. The first step in restructuring was thus to begin to change this pattern of interaction.

Aunt Rosa was clearly a critical element in the system. The therapist strategically used the information on Rosa's health as an excuse to shift some of the responsibility to the parents. The therapist tracked the family system by allying herself first with Rosa, since she had most of the power. Rosa was a superwoman, the family's gatekeeper. She had assumed much of the responsibility—too much, in fact. As a strategic intervention, the therapist argued that Rosa should slow down, be more careful about her own health, and follow her doctor's advice. This is a clear example of, first, tracking by accepting that entry into the system must be through the powerful person, and, second, reframing Rosa as a sick woman who "needs to slow down" as a way of undercutting her power. The therapist *supported* (joining technique of maintenance) Aunt Rosa's behavior and intentions, then used a theme that Aunt Rosa herself had emphasized (her poor health) to suggest that she relieve herself of the responsibilities she had imposed on herself in raising Sussy (tracking for the purpose of restructuring). Aunt Rosa still had a lot of energy and a desire to feel useful and important, however. Therefore the therapist explored with Rosa her interests and desires and how these might still be pursued outside the family and in a fashion

that was less demanding and stressful to her. As a homework assignment she continued this exploration on her own. It happened that Rosa
was a skilled seamstress and often helped her neighbors with sewing
projects. A local fabric store needed someone on a part-time basis,
partly to do alterations and partly to give advice to customers. The store
had a relaxed, friendly atmosphere. By working there Aunt Rosa could
fulfill her need to be busy and useful, but in a manner that greatly
reduced the stress on both her and the Hernandez family. She was also
able to maintain an important supportive role in the family by occasionally acting as a "consultant" to Pedro and Susana and by chaperoning
Sussy on dates and at small parties, at the request of Pedro and Susana.

The therapist then allied herself with Pedro. Pedro had a car and,
indeed, driving was one of the few things he still claimed to enjoy. The
therapist pointed out how important his driving was to the family
(tracking) and how essential this made him in this family of nondrivers
(reframing).

In getting the father to take a more active role in the family (reducing
the disengagement), the therapist also allied herself with Susana. She
explained how Pedro's more active role would also help Susana. By not
having to spend so much time worrying about Sussy, Susana was able to
get her work done more quickly and thus had more time to spend with
Sussy herself.

As an important part of this restructuring effort, the therapist directed Susana and Pedro to work as a unit in efforts to develop the
parental subsystem (creating an alliance between the spouses). She had
them discuss Sussy's problems and how to control her, as well as their
own differences regarding who had what family responsibilities. Aunt
Rosa and Sussy, of course, would frequently attempt to interrupt with
their own ideas (conflict diffusion). The therapist, however, would cut
them off immediately, thus emphasizing that the issues were executive
decisions that the parental subsystem had to make. (The therapist
blocked Rosa and Sussy's attempts at diffusion, as well their efforts at
regaining a leadership role, thereby succeeding in shifting existing
boundaries and creating new ones.) The therapist would assign Pedro
and Susana further discussions on specific topics as homework tasks.
Near the end of therapy, the parents themselves had to determine
which issues they would decide for themselves. Additionally, if they
decided to discuss it by themselves, then they also had to be the ones
who kept Aunt Rosa and Sussy out of the conversation.

In most instances, when parents cannot agree on child-rearing matters, their inability to agree is symptomatic of an underlying problem
between the spouses, such as not being able to reach compromises.

In such cases therapy must inevitably address the marital dysfunction, at least to the extent that it impinges on the couple's ability to parent effectively. While this component of the treatment is not discussed here at length, it is typically a critical aspect of any structural family work.

Finally, the therapist had to work with Sussy. Sussy wanted to get Aunt Rosa out of her life, but Sussy would have to give up some things herself. Her parents were older and more conservative than those of most of her friends. Because of this, they had attempted (though not too successfully) to be overprotective with Sussy. Out of rebellion Sussy had become extreme in her demands for freedom as well as ally with Rosa, who although far more intrusive than her parents was perceived as more liberal. The therapist pointed out to Sussy that, paradoxically, she would have to give up some of her more extreme demands in order to have more of the freedom she wanted.

The restructuring was reinforced through homework tasks designed to change interactional patterns. Pedro's role was redefined from helpless to helpful by having him assume the role of driving Aunt Rosa to the doctor's, shopping, and to her new job at the fabric store. As Sussy adopted behaviors more appropriate to her developmental stage, with the support of her parents she tried out for cheerleading. Pedro was encouraged to drive Sussy to cheerleader practice and other places as a way of bringing him closer to Sussy (reducing his disengagement) and lightening the demand on Susana's time. As part of further work on achieving a better balance of age-appropriate behaviors (developmental stage) for Sussy, a contract was achieved between Sussy and Susana by which Sussy agreed to help her mother if she wanted to get out more often, and Susana agreed to let her daughter go to more places.

When the therapist began to implement these restructuring interventions, the change precipitated a family crisis, as the family attempted to regress to its earlier homeostatic balance. All the family members had to give up some of their secondary gains, and when they were unwilling to do so, a crisis arose. Aunt Rosa began nagging Sussy again, this time about her new freedom. Sussy responded to Rosa's pressure in a typically manipulative way: She skipped school five days in a row. Pedro became depressed again and didn't want to have anything to do with Sussy. Susana used Sussy's actions to make the point that they couldn't let her have more freedom. Sussy's response was that she couldn't take it anymore. *This was the family system's effort to return to its previous pathologic homeostasis, and it is in this situation that experienced therapists' skills distinguish them from naïve therapists*; they have to help the family overcome the crisis while maintaining the gains made in therapy. These crises are usual since all systems do what they do best—maintain homeostasis. That is, family systems will do whatever is necessary to return to old familiar ways. It is extremely useful to have this regression occur during the course of therapy so that the therapist can be available to help maintain the gains. In fact, experienced therapists are likely to precipitate these crises prior to termination, if they don't occur spontaneously, in order to have the opportunity to give the family the experience once more of working itself out of the old maladaptive patterns and into more adaptive ones.

The therapist used the crisis to reinforce previous restructuring maneuvers. The therapist stood firm regarding her support for the new relational patterns. To Sussy she pointed out that if she continued to act out, the family would only attempt to be even more strict. With Pedro and Susana, she discussed Sussy's need for freedom and independence. If they attempted to overcontrol Sussy, the therapist told them, Sussy would only overreact. In their discussion Susana told the therapist, "If you give her an inch, she will take a mile." The therapist replied that Sussy would soon be a woman and that Susana had no choice but to give her "an inch" now, since it was the only realistic way to keep some contact with her daughter. Further, the therapist reinforced to the parents the relevance of their staying in the executive role and setting limits on Aunt Rosa's involvement.

With the resolution of the crisis, the restructuring phase continued until termination. At the time of termination the restructuring had been successfully accomplished. Sussy had more freedom, and her parents had more control. Sussy's friends were allowed to visit her, even though initially neither the parents nor Aunt Rosa liked them. During the restructuring the therapist encouraged the family to allow Sussy to have a party for her friends at the parents' house. Susana and Aunt Rosa helped to make the food, and Pedro helped Sussy rearrange the furniture and made sure there wasn't any trouble with the neighbors. Once the parents and Aunt Rosa got to know Sussy's friends, they became less apprehensive about them. Thus Sussy's parents had become more actively and directly involved in Sussy's life. Aunt Rosa still played an important supportive role in the family, but she no longer dominated the family. Finally, Sussy had more of the freedom that she wanted but also a more mature acceptance of the responsibility that goes with freedom.

Termination is perhaps easier in BSFT than in some other therapies, for three reasons. First, because of the time-limited nature of BSFT, termination really begins at the first session when the therapist and family establish a working contract for approximately 12 sessions. Typically, during the course of therapy the therapist will make some references to the time-limited nature of treatment, thereby continuing to prepare the family for the termination. Second, termination is made easier because the therapist does not become the primary support of any of the family members. Rather, the therapist's emphasis is on building support for family members either within the family or within the environment (as in the case of Aunt Rosa). One of the reasons that termination is difficult in most therapies is because the primary emphasis is placed on the bonding between the therapist and the patient. While in BSFT that bonding is clearly important, a tremendous emphasis is placed on directing the therapy toward strengthening bonds within the family. Hence when therapy comes to an end, family members are well supported and thus experience less distress over the loss of the therapist. Finally, termination is made easier because the therapist doesn't view the resolution of the current problems as an absolute end to the process. Rather, the BSFT therapist "leaves the door open." The family's coming back is not viewed as a failure. On the contrary, the family is encouraged to come back, much as one might visit the family doctor as the need arises.

The therapist arranged for a follow-up about 6 months after termination. Things were continuing to go well for the Hernandez family. Sussy had completely given up drug use and talked of going to the local community college after finishing high school. Aunt Rosa was proud of her job and only rarely attempted to intrude in family matters, although she was still a frequent guest. Susana had not only come to accept Sussy's friends, but one of these friends became so accepted by Susana that she spent much time at their home. Perhaps the biggest changes involved Pedro. He talked freely and smiled often. He was much closer to his wife and had developed an entirely new relationship with Sussy. While Susana and Pedro still had their differences with Sussy (she wanted to be able to stay out later and, especially, not to be chaperoned), all three had learned to discuss their differences more openly and to arrive at solutions that all three found acceptable.

Using the case of the Hernandez family, we have attempted to illustrate our systems, structural, and strategic thinking and its implementation. We have on purpose used simplistic and concrete contents to also illustrate that any content, simple though it might be, can be used in strategic and restructuring maneuvers. In fact, it is the simple, concrete contents that the family handles on a daily, routine basis that can have the greatest power both for restructuring and for generalization to similar interactions, because these simple, concrete, and routine contents are so much at the core of a family's interactions.

The reader will note that little emphasis was given to Sussy's drug use during therapy. That is because drug use, along with Sussy's other acting-out behaviors, was perceived as a symptom of a structural family problem. Hence the target of therapy was the underlying structural maladaptations. Once these were "treated," the family had the ability to bring under control Sussy's behavior problems, including the drug use.

Part IV

Breakthroughs in Engaging Resistant Families

In previous chapters we described the basic concepts of BSFT, our approach to the assessment and diagnosis of maladaptive interactions, their relationship to symptoms, and the intervention strategies characteristic of this approach. These concepts serve as the building blocks for our breakthroughs in extending strategic structural systems concepts and techniques to the engagement of resistant families.

Chapter 6 defines in structural terms the nature of the problem of resistance to entering treatment and redefines the nature of BSFT joining, diagnosing, and restructuring interventions to encompass those patterns of interactions that prevent families from coming into treatment. Chapter 7 provides case examples of the application of strategic structural systems engagement to four common types of resistant families.

6

Engagement: How to Get the Family into Therapy

José Szapocznik, Andrew L. Brickman,
Olga Hervis, and Angel Perez-Vidal

THE PROBLEM

Regardless of their theoretical orientation, mode, and place of practice, all therapists have had the disappointing and frustrating experience of "resistance to therapy" in the form of missed or cancelled first appointments. For the family therapist this becomes an even more common and complex issue, since more than one individual needs to be engaged to come to treatment.

Unfortunately, the therapist often handles this problem by accepting the resistance on the part of some family members. In effect, the

The material for this chapter was adapted from the Strategic Structural Systems Engagement Manual developed as part of a research project funded by the National Institute on Drug Abuse, Grant No. DA02059 04-06.

therapist complies with the family's definition that only one member is sick and needs treatment. Consequently, the initially well intended therapist agrees to see only one or two family members for treatment. With children and adolescents this usually results in either the child or the overwrought mother becoming the IP and following through with therapy visits.

In this case there is always the danger that the therapist has been "inducted" into the family's definition of the problem and has accepted its version of who is responsible for its difficulties. If the therapist is not alert when accepting one or two family members only, far from challenging the maladaptive patterns of interaction within the family, the therapist may unwittingly ally and reinforce the family patterns that have kept the family from resolving its problems on its own. An example is found in the case of an enmeshed mother-son relationship and peripheral father, in which the therapist accepts into therapy the mother and son, thereby reinforcing the marginality of the father.

At a more complex level, there are serious implications for the therapist who accepts the family's version of the problem. In effect, the therapist has surrendered his or her position of power. If the therapist agrees with the family's definition of "who's got the problem," her or his expertise and ability to understand the issues will be perceived by the family as no greater than its own. The therapist's credibility as a helper and the family's perception of her or his competence is at stake. Some family members may perceive the therapist as unable to challenge the status quo in the family; indeed, they may be correct. The therapist's position of power is threatened, maybe even lost.

When the therapist agrees to see only a part of the family, she or he may have surrendered too early her or his authority to orchestrate change, to move freely from one family member to another. Thus if, after beginning therapy with only a part of the family, a well intended therapist eventually attempts to interview the rest of the family, she or he will be at a great disadvantage by having begun by establishing a therapeutic relationship with only part of the family. The therapist may be perceived as having a coalition with one part of the family, and other members, in an adversarial role, may never trust her or him. At this point the therapist becomes unable to step back and observe the system as a whole, becoming a player on the stage familiar with only one of the scripts.

While some therapists respond to the resistance of full families to come to therapy by accepting those family members who most readily wish to come, other family therapists have resolved the dilemma of the resistant family by taking a more alienated stance: "There are too many motivated families waiting for help"; "the resistant families will call back when they finally feel the need"; "there is no need to get involved in a power struggle." The reality for these resistant families that are expected to come into therapy by themselves is bleak. If they are expected to come to therapy on their own, they will likely fail. Ironically, the families that most need therapy are those in which patterns and habits interfere with effective help-seeking behaviors.

A more constructive alternative for approaching resistant families is presented in this chapter. This alternative is built on the premise that resistance to coming to treatment can be understood and treated within the strategic, structural, systemic framework that we have been describing in this book. From the work previously presented, we draw on the following basic building blocks:

1. Each family system is organized into repetitive patterns of interactions.
2. Some of these patterns of interactions or structures become habitual and rigid and consequently lose their ability to adapt to new needs and situations.
3. In these families symptoms such as drug abuse may arise, and these symptoms are encouraged, maintained, and protected, albeit unwittingly, by the family's ways of interacting.

We extend these concepts to the problem of resistance to entering treatment by adding a new building block as follows:

4. When the family wishes to get rid of the symptom, such as by looking for professional help, the same interactive patterns that prevent it from getting rid of the symptom also act to prevent the family from getting help. We come to label these maladaptive interactive patterns "resistance." Yet resistance is nothing more than the family's display of its inability to adapt effectively, to help itself, or to seek help.

Thus the key to eliminating the resistance to therapy lies within the family structure; eliminate the resistance in the structure, and the family will come to therapy. Fortunately the very same principles that apply to the understanding of family functioning and treatment also apply to the understanding and "treatment" of the family's resistance to entering therapy.

A SOLUTION: ENGAGING RESISTANT FAMILIES

The techniques for engaging resistant families presented in this chapter have been developed as part of our work with BSFT. Not surprisingly, these engagement techniques use the same strategic, structural, and systemic concepts and techniques that are used during therapy, but in the case of resistant families they focus on identifying and removing the family's resistance to therapy.

In the work of overcoming resistant structures, tasks play a particularly vital role because they are the only structural strategy specifically designed to be used outside the therapist's office. Once the family is in therapy, tasks are frequently used to consolidate outside the office those gains made during the therapy sessions. Because they are designed for use outside the office, tasks are particularly well suited for use during the engagement period when crucial aspects of the family's work needs to take place outside the office, since obviously the family has not yet come in. Thus in engaging resistant families tasks are applied not to the issue of what to do with the family once it is in treatment, but rather of what to do with a family in order to get it into treatment. The central *task* around which we organize the entire process of engagement is that of "coming together" to therapy.

The Task of Coming to Therapy

The therapist gives to the family member who calls for help the task of bringing the whole family in to therapy. The therapist explains why this is a good idea, with the usual promises of support. Occasionally this is all that is needed. Often people do not request family therapy simply because family therapy is not well known, and thus it does not occur to them to take such action. Sometimes there's fear of what will happen. Some of these fears may be real; others may be simply imagined. In some instances, some families may respond to reassuring advice that overcomes their apprehension. Having overcome their apprehension, they are now ready to come to therapy.

Very often, however, simple clarification and reassurance is not sufficient to mobilize a family. What is needed at this point are directives to undertake tasks that attempt to change the ways in which family members act with one another, and in the process expose the family's resistances. When directives to change fail and resistances are exposed, then the therapist will have the information needed on the basis of which to do needed restructuring in order to get the family into therapy.

Thus when assigning any task, the therapist must expect that the task may not be performed as requested. This is certainly the case for the task involving asking the family to come together to therapy. Tasks represent direct and sensible actions that relatively well functioning people and families can take to correct the unpleasant situations about which they complain. For instance, the therapist may give a mother the task of discussing with her husband his participation in therapy on Tuesday in order to bring their rebellious 15-year-old son who is using drugs and skipping school. The implication in the task is that the mother and father will work cooperatively and effectively to achieve their son's adherence to their decision. If it were that simple, the family would probably not need to come to therapy at all. It would already possess the requisite family interactive skills necessary to control the child. Hence it is important that the therapist be prepared to encounter obstacles in accomplishing tasks and that she or he *define failure to accomplish these tasks in much the same way as she or he defines obstacles to the accomplishment of other therapeutic tasks: with patience and ingenuity.*

Obstacles to accomplishing the tasks involved in bringing the family into therapy can be viewed as avoidance based on the family's efforts to maintain its homeostasis (i.e., the system's natural tendency is to attempt to perpetuate its maladaptive interactions). The inability or unwillingess to come to therapy always has its roots in the family's patterns of interactions. Obstacles to coming to therapy must therefore be explored in a way that uncovers (diagnosis) and overcomes (restructures) this resistance. How is this to be done?

The strategies to be used during engagement to overcome the family's resistance to therapy are similar to the joining, diagnosing, and restructuring techniques used during therapy. The application of these techniques to the engagement of resistant families is discussed separately below. As occurs in therapy, however, these techniques of joining, diagnosis, and restructuring occur simultaneously during engagement and are often intermixed.

JOINING

Joining the resistant family is a process that begins with the very first contact with the family member who calls for help and continues throughout the entire experience with the family. Thus in engaging resistant families we have extended the concept of joining from a process that begins with the first family session to a process that begins with the very first contact with the therapist. Hence it is often necessary to "join" the family through the person who initially calls for help.

With resistant families the joining techniques described earlier have to be modified to match the aims of this phase of therapy, namely, that of overcoming resistance. In tracking a resistant family in order to get them engaged, for example, it is necessary to track through the caller or initial help seeker and any other members who may conjointly or sequentially involve themselves in the process of bringing the family to therapy. Since this often results in the therapist's not seeing the whole family at once, the actual interactions may not be self-evident at first glance. However, in this case the therapist tracks by "following" from the first family member to the next available and the next, and so forth. This "following" or tracking is done without challenging the structure and by permitting the structure to open up its available doors and let the therapist in.

Establishing a Therapeutic Alliance

A very effective way to establish a therapeutic alliance is for the therapist to say to the resistant members that she or he knows they want to solve *their* problems and that the therapist wants the same thing. It must be recognized, however, that how the problem is defined may vary from one member to another. For example, the mother may want to get her son to quit drugs, while the son may want to get his mother off his back. When the therapist and the family members agree on a goal, therapy is offered as a framework for achieving that goal. Even when family members are in conflict over their aims, it is necessary to find some gain for each of them to be achieved from therapy. For example, the therapist can say to the mother that her son should stop using drugs; to the son, that his mother should get off his back and stop her nagging; and to the father, that he should stop being called in constantly to referee or play "bad guy." In each case the therapist can offer therapy as a means for each family member to achieve the goal of getting rid of the problem (which in each case is defined differently).

In engaging resistant families the therapist works with and through only one or a few family members. Because the entire family is not initially available, the therapist will need to form a bond with the caller and any other family members that make themselves available initially. The focus of work during this early engagement phase will be to work with these persons in order to bring about the changes necessary to engage the entire family in therapy. By using the contact person as a vehicle (via tracking) for joining with other various members of the family, the therapist can eventually establish a therapeutic alliance with each family member and thereby elicit the cooperation of the entire family in the engagement effort.

DIAGNOSIS

Diagnosis involves identifying the nature of the relationship between maladaptive patterns and undesirable symptoms. In the case of resistant families, the undesirable symptom is defined as the family's inability or unwillingness to come into treatment. Similarily, the maladaptive patterns of interaction that are of interest to the therapist during the engagement process are those that are maintaining or promoting the resistant behavior.

In engagement the purpose of diagnosis is to identify those patterns of interaction that are permitting the resistant behavior to manifest itself. Because it is impossible to administer the Family Tasks until the entire family comes into treatment, the therapist of necessity works with very limited information to diagnose the patterns of interactions that are supporting the resistance. In order to identify the maladaptive patterns responsible for the resistance, we have extended the use of the informal diagnosis forward to begin, prior to therapy, with the first phone contact by a family member. Beyond the impossibility of administering the Family Tasks prior to engagement, it is not even possible to encourage and observe enactments of the conjoint family interactions. Thus the informal diagnosis has been modified for use during engagement to collect the assessment information in other ways. Two ways that we have found useful in our work follow.

First, the contact person can be asked questions, allowing us to infer what the interactional patterns may be. For example, "How do you ask your husband to come to treatment?" "What happens when you ask your husband to come to treatment?" "And when he gets angry at you for asking him to come to treatment, what do you do next?" In this way we seek to identify the circular patterns of causality that may be contributing to the resistance. The wife, for example, might be asking the husband to come to treatment in an accusatory way, which causes him to get angry.

Second, the therapist can explore the family system for resistances to the central task of coming to therapy. This effort is accomplished by assigning exploratory tasks in order to uncover resistances that might cause the family to fail at the task of coming into therapy. For example, in the case above the therapist might suggest to the wife that she ask her husband to come for her sake, not because there is anything wrong with him. The wife then says to the therapist, "I can't really ask him for my sake, because I know he's so busy that it's just not fair." Thus it would appear that the wife is ambivalent about getting the husband to come to treatment. On the one hand, she claims to want him to come into treatment, but on the other, she gives excuses for why he shouldn't. The purpose of exploring the resistance beginning with the first phone call is to identify as early as possible potential obstacles to coming into therapy, with the aim of intervening in a way that gets around these obstacles.

In the process of working with the caller, the therapist asks clarifying questions, evidences interest in the family, and supports existing patterns of behavior. As patterns of behavior become apparent, the therapist uses this information to make an informal assessment and diagnosis. This diagnosis can then be depicted using a family structural map. While mapping is always useful in depicting the structure of a family, it is particularly useful in engagement because more rigorous assessment and diagnosis procedures (i.e., the formal and the semiformal approaches) are totally unavailable. Thus the informal approach to diagnosis is used to identify the structural relations impacting on resistance to therapy, and engagement maps are used to help depict these structures. In particular, engagement maps are used in helping to depict the four types of resistant families described later in this chapter (see pp. 87–91). Using engagement maps, the therapist can follow the flow of family interaction, thereby identifying the family structure and positioning herself or himself as a leader of the newly formed therapeutic system.

What makes this type of early diagnostic work possible is an understanding of the principle of complementarity described in more detail in Chapters 1 and 8. As noted in these chapters, for a family to work as a unit (even though maladaptively), the behaviors of each family member must "fit in" with the behavior of each and every other family member. Thus, within the family, for each action there is a complementary action or reaction. For example, the husband doesn't want to come into treatment (the action), and the wife excuses him from not coming into treatment (the complementary action). Similarly, when a caller tells the therapist that whenever she says anything to her husband about therapy (the action) he becomes angry (the complementary reaction), the therapist needs to ascertain if there is anything that the wife did to elicit an angry response. We seek for the circular causality because, as we know, the behaviors of members of a family are like the inner workings of a clock: For the clock to keep functioning, all the wheels must turn in a certain way. Similarly, for the family to continue to function or dysfunction in a certain way, everyone's behavior must contribute to maintaining the family's pattern of behavior.

RESTRUCTURING

In the process of engaging resistant families, the therapist initially sees only one or a few of the members of the family. It is still possible, through these individuals, to bring about changes in interactive patterns that will allow the family to come for therapy. A variety of change-producing interventions have already been described in Chapter 5, including reframing, reversals, detriangulation, opening up closed systems, shifting alliances, and task setting. All of these techniques can be used by the therapist to overcome the family's resistance to therapy. In the process of engaging resistant families, task setting is as useful in restructuring as it is in joining and diagnosis. In the next section we discuss the types of resistant families that we have identified, the process of getting the family into therapy (identifying the resistance and restructuring the interactive patterns contributing to the resistance), and the central role that tasks may play in achieving this goal.

TYPES OF RESISTANT FAMILIES

Our work with resistant families has been done with Hispanic families in the Miami area, where the family adolescent was known or believed by the parents to be either using drugs or engaging in behaviors associated with the use of drugs, such as truancy, delinquency, aggressiveness, frequent fights in and outside the home, keeping "bad company," and coming home very late at night. These families provide an example of the types of families that are difficult to engage in therapy. However, the examples are not intended to represent all possible types of structural configurations that work to resist therapy. Therapists working with other types of problems and families are encouraged to review their caseload of "difficult to engage" families and to carefully examine the clues for diagnosing the systemic resistances to therapy. You may find that they are similar to those we have found, or you may find them very different. In any case, you will be better equipped to deal with these families if you have some understanding of the types of resistances that are typical of your caseload.

There have been four general structural organizations that have emerged repeatedly in our work with families of drug-abusing adolescents who present engagement resistance to therapy. These four patterns are discussed below in terms of what becomes evident to the therapist as the mechanisms of resistance go into effect.

Powerful Identified Patient

The most frequently observed type of resistance to enter treatment is characterized by a powerful IP. These families have within their structure a powerful IP and parents who are hierarchically positioned at a lower level of power relative to the IP. The salient characteristic of parental power at the initial stages of engagement is the ability of the parents to bring the child to therapy without lying to the child. Very often the mother of a powerful IP will admit that she is weak or ineffective and will say that her son or daughter flatly refuses to come to therapy. We can assume that the IP resists therapy because:

1. It threatens his position of power and moves him to a "problem-person" position.
2. It is the parent's agenda to come to therapy, and thus if followed it will enhance the parent's power.

Restructuring needs to be done to alter the existing hierarchical organization in which the IP is in power, thereby eliminating the resistance to initial engagement. In these cases the hierarchical organization is altered not by "demoting" the IP (that move would be totally rejected at first) but rather by allying the therapist to the "ruling structure." The therapist brings respect and concern for the IP but also an agenda of change that will then, by virtue of the alliance, be shared by the IP.

In order to bring these families into treatment, the IP's hierarchical position is not directly challenged but tracked and allied to the therapist so that the therapist may later be in a position to interject her or his formulation and solution to the problem (i.e., restructure). Therefore the therapist forms an alliance with the powerful IP in order to reframe the need for therapy in a manner that strengthens the IP in a positive way. The reframing is done so that the symptom is transferred from the IP to the family (further supporting the IP's power, to be later challenged in therapy). The other alternative, that of forming an alliance with the parents, would be premature and ineffective at the early stage of the engagement process. The parental subsystem is not strong enough at this point. The pressure to perform while the therapist has no direct access to the IP would render the parents even weaker, and the family would "disappear."

Contact Person Protecting Structure

The second most common type of resistance to entering treatment is characterized by a parent who protects the structure. In these families the person making the agency contact (usually the mother) is also the person overprotecting the resistant behavior. How the IPhood is maintained in the family is also how therapy is resisted. The mother gives a double message to the therapist: "I want to take my family to therapy, but my son can't come because he forgot and fell asleep, and my husband has so much work he can't take any time to come to therapy." The mother is expressing a desire for the therapist's help while at the same time protecting and allying with the family's resistance to being involved in solving the problem. The mother "protects" this resistance by agreeing that the excuses for noninvolvement in change are valid. In other words, she is supporting the arguments used for maintaining the status quo. It is worthwhile to note that ordinarily this is the same double-bind in the family that perpetuates the symptomatic structure; someone complains of the problem behavior yet supports the maintenance of the problem. This pattern is typical of the family whose patterns of resistance are closely tied to a problem of enmeshment between the mother and the IP.

In order to bring these families into treatment, the therapist must first form an alliance with the mother by acknowledging her frustration in wanting to get help and not getting any cooperation from the family member(s). Through this alliance the therapist then moves to the other members and distances them from the mother, such that the therapist can challenge the mother's position of resistance once the therapist has a relationship with other family members.

Disengaged Parent

These family structures are characterized by little or no cohesiveness or alliance between the parents as a subsystem. In addition, one of the parents (usually the father) refuses to go to therapy. This is typically a parent who has remained disengaged from the problematic behavior. This additional resistance serves to disengage him from another problematic relationship: the other spouse. Typically the mother is overinvolved with the IP and either incompetent in parenting or supporting the IPhood in a covert fashion. For example, if the father moves in to control the behavior, she complains he's too tough or creates mythical fears about the father's potential violence. Thus the father is rendered useless and again moves out, re-establishing the disengagement between husband and wife. In this family the dimension of resonance is of foremost importance in planning change to bring it to therapy. The mother must be brought closer to the father in tasks that distance her from the son. As noted earlier, resonance is that measure of closeness/ distance that qualifies any relationship. The closer the relationship (enmeshed), the higher the degree of sensitivity for each other; conversely, the greater the distance (disengaged), the lower will be the awareness of the other.

In order to engage these families in treatment, the therapist must form an alliance with the caller (usually the mother). The therapist then begins to direct the mother's interactions with the father, changing their patterns of interaction so as to bring him into therapy. The therapist gives mother tasks to do together with her husband pertaining *only* to the issue of taking care of their son's problems. This is done because it must be assumed that if the father and mother have become distanced, there must be a conflict of some intensity between them. For this reason the therapist attempts to ensure the insulation of the broader conflict until the marital couple is ready to confront it. These tasks are intended to restructure their interaction only around the problem youth and in a way that stimulates the father to accept coming to therapy.

Although the pattern is similar to that of the contact person protecting the structure, in this instance the resistance emerges differently. In this case the mother does not excuse the father's distance, but, quite the contrary, she complains about her spouse's disinterest; the mother is usually more willing to do something, given some direction.

Therapy as an Exposé

Sometimes therapy is threatening to one or more individuals. They resist coming because they are afraid of being made a scapegoat or that dangerous secrets will be revealed. These individuals' beliefs or "frames" about therapy are usually an extension of the "frame" within which the family is functioning.

The therapist must reframe the idea or goal of therapy in a way that eliminates its negative consequences and replaces them with positive aims. This must be done for the member(s) of the family who are being victimized or threatened by therapy.

In reviewing these patterns it is evident that in mobilizing a family for therapy, considerably more changes are needed in some types of families than in others. For example, families with disengaged parents require more complex work than families in which the contact person is protecting the structure. In turn, the latter type of family needs more work than the one protecting a family secret, where a simple reframing from a position of close therapeutic alliance will do the job. Therefore the notion of degree of change needed by different types of resistant families becomes a highly relevant issue, though not unlike the already accepted reality that some families in therapy need more thorough and deeper restructuring than others.

In reviewing our approaches to overcoming resistance to treatment, the ethics of engaging into treatment individuals and/or families who are hesitant or perhaps resistant to becoming involved ought to be considered. This general concern about the ethics of therapeutic strategies is as old as therapy itself. From the earliest times most therapies have been developed on what may be referred to as *the therapeutic paradox*. That is, the therapist accepts the client/patient in order to gain the client/patient's trust, with the ultimate goal of fomenting change in the now trusting client/patient. Hence the paradox: I accept you to change you. Our approach to engaging resistant families takes advantage of this well known paradox, accepting the family system (joining and tracking) in order to overcome their resistant interactions (restructuring).

This therapeutic paradox, as used generally and as used in our own approach, is to some extent manipulative in that the therapist accepts the client/patient in order to gain entry and in turn gains entry in order to bring about change. The crucial ethical concern, however, is not with the use of the paradox or the concomitant apparent manipulation. Rather, the ethical concern revolves around the extent to which the therapist, by using the paradox, either coerces the client/patient to move in a predetermined direction or, alternatively, merely creates the conditions that free the client/patient from automatic and habitual behaviors, thereby promoting new, more adjusted choices.

While the therapist makes some assumptions about the general direction in which a client/patient should move from pathologic behaviors to those behaviors that are personally and socially more adjusted, what is critically important is that the therapist is never coercive—that the actual choices for change are always left to the client/patient. As illustrated in the next chapter, as we take each step, we ask the relevant family member for permission to take that step. Hence the process on a step-by-step basis has the approval of the family.

In the next chapter we will walk through typical case histories involving the four types of resistant families and describe our approach to treatment in each case.

7

Engagement: Some Clinical Examples

José Szapocznik, Angel Perez-Vidal,
Olga Hervis, and Andrew L. Brickman

In this chapter we illustrate how we have applied our specialized engagement techniques in actual practice. One case study is presented for each of the four types of resistant families outlined in the previous chapters. We begin with the type of case we have encountered most frequently.

CASE I: POWERFUL IDENTIFIED PATIENT RESISTS THERAPY

The Ñunez Family

Identified Patient:	Raul, age 18
Father:	Juan, age 40
Stepmother:	Mirta, age 39
Stepmother's lover:	Victoria, age 32

BACKGROUND

Raul was the only identified patient in a family with multiple problems. His reaction to this "injustice" was to extol a price for assuming the "bad guy" position. His price, by virtue of his age and being male in a Latin family, was to demand total independence from any parental authority. He assumed a "tough" stance that seemed impenetrable to his family members. Raul used cocaine and marijuana and openly disregarded parental authority. His attitude at home was defiant and disruptive.

Being identified as the patient was painful enough, but having that experience in a family with obvious multiple problems was experienced as even more unfair and consequently increased the level of aggression and rebelliousness.

First, his natural mother left him. Then his father left him to the father's second wife (Raul's stepmother) when they divorced. He had been recently kicked out of his stepmother's home. Raul had historically experienced abandonment. Abandonment again was almost intolerable.

Juan was Raul's natural father. He raised Raul with his second wife, Mirta. When they divorced, Mirta assumed the care of Raul, although she frequently would send Raul to his father when she became overwhelmed in attempting to cope with Raul. Juan would take him in for a few days to convince Mirta and Raul that he should return to Mirta's house. Juan was particularly desperate because neither Raul nor Mirta were budging and he (Juan) could not handle Raul any longer. Juan had remarried a third time after divorcing Mirta. However, he was now separated and lived alone for the last 2 years.

Mirta was Raul's stepmother. She had "tried hard" but could not take Raul anymore. She lived in a lesbian relationship with a woman who had little patience or interest in Raul. Mirta raised Raul from age 2 when she married Juan. Raul had lived in Mirta's home since she left Juan 7 years later.

Victoria was Mirta's lover. She had been in Raul's life for approximately 4 years and had no power in relation to Raul.

The family was chaotic by virtue of two divorces, three remarriages, and four "parental" figures and their obvious inability to keep any order or structure. Often these situations place the offspring in a rather powerful position (like "power by default") at an early age, given the inadequacy and incompetence of the parents. The IP was both resented and feared, thus increasing his inner sense of worthlessness, giving way to acting out and anger. Raul had no allies in this family; he was in a powerful but lonely position. The parents were playing ping pong to see who could avoid being the parent. Meanwhile, Raul was unguided, unsupported, and unstructured.

SUMMARY OF CONTACTS[1]

1/31/84
Juan called the Center, requesting help for his son, Raul. He explained that his son had been kicked out of the stepmother's home and had come to live with him. Juan did not want this arrangement to continue. In passing, he mentioned his concern that Raul was using drugs. It was evident that Juan's main issue was that Raul was disrupting Juan's life.

> *Actually, Juan was asking help for himself, as he did not want Raul in his home. The fact was that Raul had been having problems for some time and only now that he had moved in with Juan did the father mobilize.*

The therapist scheduled an appointment for the next day, after having reassured the father of his willingness and ability to help the family get through the crisis. The therapist requested that Raul, Juan, and Mirta be present.

> *The central task of "bringing the family to therapy" was initially given to Juan.*

2/1/84
The family did not show up for the appointment and did not call to cancel or to explain. The therapist attempted to reach Juan, to no avail.

> *The failure of Juan in accomplishing this central task opened the opportunity to explore the family's resistance. The therapist needed to extend his help quickly to utilize the crisis as a mobilizing force.*

2/1/84
Later in the afternoon, not being able to reach Juan, the therapist called Mirta. She said, "Dr. P. V., it's impossible to get Raul to go there. He claims he's not crazy and says he doesn't want to be bothered anymore."

---

[1]Events and observations are followed by comments and explanations in italics.

Strategically, the therapist used not being able to reach Juan as an excuse to call Mirta and join her.

Raul, understandably, rebelled against being "officially" labeled as the IP.

The therapist reassured Mirta by saying, "Well, that's a pretty common reaction among these youngsters."

When Mirta expressed her hopelessness, the therapist minimized Raul's behavior, as a way of supporting Mirta, by pointing out that she was not alone because many parents confront the same problem. Support is a joining strategy.

She quickly interrupted by saying, "No, you've got Raul all wrong. When he says it's no, then it's no. He is hard as a rock, and there's no talking to him."

Within the first 5 min of a conversation with Mirta, Mirta provided critically important information toward the diagnosis. Raul was powerful, and when he took a position, his parents could not easily move him to do otherwise.

Again the therapist minimized the conflict and nature of Raul's statement. "I know, I know. It always seems that way at first, but eventually we find a way to 'soften them up.' Don't give up hope, Mirta, but do help me." Mirta said, "What do you mean? You're the one who should help me."

The therapist provided further support while making efforts to engage Mirta in a therapeutic alliance.

"Well," said Dr. P. V., "we have to help each other. That is, you have to help me so that I can help you and Raul." Mirta asked, "How am I supposed to do that? He won't listen to me." The therapist then asked Mirta to help him reach Raul directly.

The therapist tracked the communication pathways to the IP through the stepmother. That is, the therapist followed the lines of communication in the family as they were laid out.
The therapist needed to reach Raul, either through the stepmother or the father, to create a therapeutic alliance that initially respected his independence and power in content yet altered the

process by placing a powerful person (the therapist), who has a different process agenda, in an allied position to the IP. This new and also powerful ally (the expert therapist) will eventually advocate for the parental agenda for change in the IP's behavior from a position inside the power structure.

Mirta claimed that it was really the father's problem now, since Raul was living with Juan. "True, but I think Juan needs your help and if the two of you work it right together, you can help me to reach Raul." The therapist needed to shift the game between parents from "ping pong" to mutual cooperation.

Mirta agreed to talk to Juan about it to see how they could "get around" Raul's anger and get him to talk to Dr. P. V. The therapist made a suggestion: "I'll tell you what. The first thing to do is to stop making Raul feel like the black sheep and, instead, present it to him more as the whole family needing help to figure this out."

The therapist coached the family to move from a position of negativity about Raul as being the only person with a problem to spreading the problem around so that all family members could share some part of the responsibility. This lessened the rigidity of Raul's IPhood and thus permitted Raul to lower his defensive, angry stance.

Mirta began to protest this stance and became defensive, but the therapist quickly reassured her that this was a necessary "twist." Whether or not it was true was not important. What was important was that Raul would be less angry and therefore easier to bring to therapy.

2/6/84

Mirta called the therapist. She disscussed it, as planned, with Juan, and she now felt it was best if the therapist would talk to Juan directly. The therapist thanked Mirta and agreed with her.

The initial call for help had come from Juan. However, the therapist had sensed that Mirta would be more involved, and hence the therapist had moved to establish an initial therapeutic alliance with Mirta. Now, through Mirta, the therapist tracked back to Juan. This pattern of interactions, placing Mirta in a more central parenting role than Juan, reflects the way the family usually operates.

2/6/84

The therapist called Juan. Juan claimed there was no way he could get Raul to come to the clinic and suggested that perhaps Dr. P. V. could come to the house. "I can't guarantee he'll even talk to you, but we've got a better chance that way."

> *There was now a cooperative therapeutic team formed by father-mother-therapist.*

The therapist agreed with Juan and again suggested that this visit should be announced to Raul, rather than "sneaking up" on him, and, most importantly, suggested an explanation: "Say to Raul that you asked me to come here to help you, Juan, to learn how to better help yourself and your son."

> *In order to join a powerful IP, the therapist must be willing to meet the IP on his own turf. The therapist asked to be announced, as a way of showing Raul that he was respected and considered, thus tracking his powerful role.*

The father agreed to the plan.

> *Again, it was important to continue deemphasizing Raul's role as "the patient." The therapist got the parents to cooperate because he "sold" this strategy as effective in bringing Raul to therapy.*

2/7/84

Juan called and said that he followed Dr. P. V.'s advice, and Raul agreed to be present at the visit next evening at 7:00 P.M.

2/8/84

The therapist arrived at Juan's home on time. Juan was living in a cramped efficiency apartment. The therapist asked Juan to introduce him to Raul.

> *The therapist tracked Juan's "official" position as head of the family and used it to move to Raul.*

As he shook hands with Raul, he said, "I want to thank you for making this time to meet with me."

> *The therapist's highest priority was to join with Raul in a manner that maintained Raul's position of power.*

Dr. P. V. continued, "I have spoken to both your mother and father on the phone, but I am sure that you have your own opinions about what's been happening and about how I can best be of help."

The therapist made it clear to Raul that Raul's opinions were of utmost importance and not to be ignored.

"That's why it was so important for me to meet with you personally," said Dr. P. V. Raul was at first somewhat clumsy about dealing with the therapist, so the latter quickly helped by saying, "Tell you what, just tell me a little bit about how you see the situation with your family."

Raul's position of power had been attained by rebelliousness, inability of the parents to control him, and aggressiveness, but this time, it was given to him out of concern and respect for his feelings. The experience of importance shifted from "negative" to "positive."

At this point, Raul offered the therapist a drink, and the therapist replied jokingly, "No, thank you, there's too many calories in booze, and I'm already too fat. Did you know that they say drinking after dinner is what puts the most weight on you?" Raul told the therapist that in that case, he'll never get fat because he does not drink. Then he pointed to his father, who was having a drink, and commented, "They criticize me about using drugs, but you can see they like to booze it up instead." The therapist responded, "Well, you may have a point there, Raul, but I'm really here to see how I can help you, not to analyze your father's drinking habits."

The therapist, who saw Raul's attempt at triangulating him, managed to maintain an allied position to Raul without distancing the father.

He quickly then moved to ask Raul about how terrible it must be to be made to feel like the "black sheep."

The therapist by this acknowledged Raul's attempts to have the therapist see his pain in being scapegoated. This joining encouraged Raul to continue talking.

Raul agreed and commented how sick and tired he was of hearing nothing but complaints about him and of being pressured about getting a job, going to school, and so on. The therapist listened patiently and for quite a while to Raul's complaints about the parents and finally suggested, "Look, Raul, you have convinced me that the situation is not as simple as you should just stop drugs and get a job. I can see that there are many feelings and issues involved here and that although your parents want what's best for you, perhaps they're going about this all wrong. Actually, I'm sure that the worse they make you feel, the less you'll want to make some positive changes."

This was a way to join Raul in content (by agreeing that the problem was much bigger than Raul) while joining the parents in the process (encouraging Raul to come into treatment). Content is what people say, and process is defined in terms of behavior. Thus the therapist agreed with Raul's content while getting Raul to behave as his parent wanted him to, that is, to come to treatment. This "dance" between content and process as well as between family members is useful in creating a conjoint therapeutic system.

Dr. P. V. said, "So perhaps you can agree with me that the best way for me to be able to help you is for all of us together to work at sifting this out in the office so we can come to some reasonable compromises that can make everyone happy and nicer to each other. So tell me, do we have a deal? If you help me, I'll help you." Raul agreed to come to the office with his parents the next day. A call was placed to the mother, and she agreed to come to the clinic also.

The therapist had made it evident that the problem was with the whole family. The negativity of Raul is lessened, thus rendering him more amenable to therapy. The diagnosis of the nature of the resistance to coming to therapy had revealed that the powerful IP refused to come to therapy. The solution to the problem was to reach the IP directly, to join the IP, and to provide him with an incentive to come to therapy while lessening the family forces that were causing the IP to be negative (i.e., the family's focusing all blame on Raul).

2/9/86

Raul arrived at the clinic with Juan. Mirta arrived 15 min later. During the 1st hour, the following information was revealed to the therapist, either directly or by observation: (1) Because Raul had just recently moved to the father's home, having lived most of his life with his stepmother, the father-son relationship was very weak. (2) It was only a matter of time before Raul would be expelled from the father's home due to space limitations and the increased tension caused by his presence. (3) The home in which Raul was raised consisted of his stepmother and her female lover.

The opportunity to observe the family in vivo *allowed for a more thorough diagnosis of family interactions. A weak father–son relationship was observed, as well as a conflicted relationship between Juan and Mirta around child-rearing issues. Both of these maladaptive interactions provided a framework for determining what restructuring would be needed in treatment.*

The therapist questioned Mirta about her reasons for kicking Raul out of her home. He commented, "That certainly is a radical move, given all the time, effort, and interest you've invested in Raul over the years."

The therapist supported Mirta by recognizing her feelings and dedication and at the same time invited her to question her decision to kick Raul out. If Mirta allied with the position that the therapist was voicing, this would constitute a shift in Mirta's position vis-à-vis Raul.

Mirta agreed with the therapist that she had tried very hard, but claimed she finally got fed up, felt hopeless about Raul changing his ways, and had to come to this decision. The therapist joined with Mirta emotionally; "It must have been so hard for you, because it's obvious that you care a lot for this boy. I mean, a natural mother may put up with a lot because she's supposed to, but you had a choice and you chose to love and care for Raul without an obligation. That's real love in my book." Mirta agreed and started to cry. The therapist interjected, "Well, maybe if you hadn't felt so hopeless you would not have done this." Mirta said, "That's right." She didn't know what to do, and she couldn't be a party to his ruining his life and also affecting her current relationship and family. The therapist agreed with this position but interjected that he did not feel this was hopeless but rather merely "misdirected."

The therapist then proposed, "Well, if we can get an arrangement going here that is acceptable to all, perhaps Raul can move back to Mirta's home, and we will all continue to work in therapy to resolve the various difficulties.

The therapist proposed a negotiation that supported Raul's need for structure and nurturance while offering the family his continued presence and involvement, that is, a new structure wherein the "old system" was strengthened and restructured by the presence of the therapist in the task of reconstructing the family.

Mirta said she would only consider this if Raul agreed to keep coming to therapy. Before Raul could answer, the therapist moved close to Raul and said, "Well, I feel pretty certain that Raul will continue to come and see me, because we've hit it off very well.

The therapist quickly moved in close alliance with Raul in order to ensure getting Raul's cooperation.

Dr. P. V. said, "It took the whole family to get things to where they are, and it'll take the whole family to get it together again. I need all of you to commit yourselves to coming to therapy. We won't always be working all together at the same time, but we'll take turns."

Now that the initial resistance to entering therapy had been overcome, the family was ready to begin therapy. Again the therapist decentralized Raul as "sole" patient and spread the problem throughout the whole system. This maneuver further supported Raul.

Dr. P. V. continued, "Juan and Raul need to work out some good feelings together, which every boy wants from his father. On the other hand, Mirta and Raul need to come to terms on some reasonable rules that will help make the home environment agreeable to all of you. These kinds of things we'll work out on separate sessions. So how about it?

The therapist described the therapy contract, which respected the boundaries between the two families and between people. He also began to identify for the family what the "other" problems were. That is called "moving to a new symptom," and as a restructuring technique it challenges the family's maladaptive organization around the IP.

Dr. P. V. asked, "I know (correct me if I'm wrong, Raul) I've got a deal with Raul, but how about the rest of you? Are you as willing to give it your all as he is?" The family agreed to commit to therapy. Raul agreed to move back to Mirta's home over the weekend. Raul and Mirta agreed that both of them along with Victoria would come in to negotiate some structure next Monday afternoon.

2/12/86
Raul, Mirta, and Victoria came in for intake and first therapy session.

The therapist chose to begin therapy with Raul's "everyday" family because its structuring was critical to holding Raul in therapy.

CASE II: CONTACT PERSON PROTECTS RESISTANT STRUCTURE

The Suarez Family

Identified Patient: Eddy, age 17
    Father: Eduardo, age 48
    Mother: Marta, age 44
    Sisters: Elena, age 23, and Blanca, age 21

4/9/84

The mother called the clinic stating her concern that her 17-year-old son was using cocaine and marijuana. The therapist gave the mother support by listening to a lengthy exposition of her anguish and fears about how her son was going to end up. A prompt appointment for later that week was offered to reinforce the clinic's concern and willingness to help.

> *The therapist allowed all the time necessary for the mother to express herself, as a technique aimed at immediately starting a supportive alliance. It was also a way of uncovering relevant family data that permitted the therapist to begin developing a Family Map.*

The mother was told that the whole family needed to come. The mother answered in a subdued tone, "Well, I'll see what I can do. My husband and daughters are so busy all the time." The therapist reiterated that the help and involvement of the whole family was most needed and beneficial in treating the situation.

> *The central task of coming to therapy was given to the mother. Immediately, the mother began to provide excuses for her husband and daughters, hence revealing potentially important diagnostic information about the nature of the resistance.*

4/10/84

The mother called the therapist to apologize because she had to cancel the appointment; no one in the family could come. "Won't you reconsider and just see my son and me?" She asked the therapist. The mother added that her son prefered to come by himself anyway. When asked by the therapist if he could talk to the son directly, the mother explained, "Well, he's not in now, but whatever you and I negotiate will be okay with him." The therapist said, "Well, I'm sure you know your son best, but it's been my experience that most young men this age resent it if they're taken for granted and if they're not consulted and, as I'm sure you know, if I'm going to help him I better make sure that he doesn't start angry at me." "Also," the therapist continued, "I would like to ask him how he feels about his father being involved in his therapy; maybe he can find a way to get his father to come in."

The mother's speaking for the son was a sign of an enmeshed relationship. Such relationships are generally laden with ambivalent love/hate feelings and in this case kept the third party, the father, distant from both mother and son. It was obvious that if the therapist "bought" mother's recommendation, he would be tacitly accepting the very structure that served to maintain the symptom(s). The father would then stay away from therapy, and the son would see therapy as another of the mother's continuous attempts to control him. Therapy would reinforce the established familial pattern in which the spousal conflicts of the parents were set aside and ignored in deference to the purported dysfunction of the son. This is called "conflict detouring." By obviating the mother's recommendation, the therapist challenged the maladaptive structure (as it was protected by the centralized mother) and opened up new avenues of interaction that were dyadic (not triadic) and direct (not through another person). In many cases the son's acting out is an attempt to both gain independence from the mother and to get the father's attention.

Marta hemmed and hawed, then quickly pointed out, "The problem is that my husband is rarely home before 10:00 P.M., and I don't think he'll ever be able to take off time to come." As to the son, "He's not home now."

The therapist suggested perhaps he could help her, since she is "so concerned and obviously not getting much cooperation from the rest of the family," by talking to the rest of the members directly. The mother was hesitant. The therapist said, "I hear some fears on your part for me to do this. Maybe I can help to reassure you that my only concern is to help your family see how important it is that we all work together in resolving your son's drug problem."

A therapist was perhaps tempted here to begin to develop some negative reactions to the mother, who on the one hand asks for help and on the other makes help difficult. The family therapist recognized that this was the double-bind message that the mother needed to send even within her own family, to keep the system's homeostatic balance (symptomatic as it may have been). The therapist offered his help not by challenging the mother but by choosing to ally only with her intended purpose and by being apparently oblivious to her resistant maneuvers. This alliance strengthened the "help and change" side of her double message.

Slowly but surely, the therapist, with warmth and patience, was able to convince the mother that he would be most tactful and gentle with the family, and she agreed to help the therapist talk to the father and son directly.

The father would be contacted at home by phone in the evening, and the son would be met by the therapist after school in the schoolyard. The therapist, tracking the structure, asked the mother to be in charge of arranging these contacts with the father for that evening and her son for next afternoon.

Paradoxically, the therapist gave the mother, who was very central in this system, the task of giving the therapist direct access to other family members.

4/10/84 (evening)

The therapist called the home and spoke to the father, verbalizing the mother's great fears and concerns for their son's drug abuse and general emotional state. Initially, the father was angry in tone. "I've had enough of hearing about his problems. He's 17 years old, and if he wants to ruin his life, there's nothing I can do about it." The therapist fully empathized with the father's sense of hopelessness (not the overt anger), saying, "Eduardo, I know how you must feel seeing your son going down the drain and feeling that you can't do anything to stop it. However I want to tell you that there is a lot you can do, with my help, and there's nothing I can do without yours."

The therapist strategically brought to focus the father's desperation and purposefully moved away from the anger in order to strengthen the caring functions (and weaken the rejecting behavior). Thus the therapist joined with that part of the father that cared. The therapist reframed the father's position from one of powerlessness to one of power (more powerful than the professional expert).

Eduardo at first continued to resist, but in lessening degree as the therapist continued to offer him hope, strength, and guidance because "at 17, Eddy needs you more than he needs his own mother."

The therapist acknowledged his awareness that the triangle (Eddy-mother-father) had kept Eddy away from his father, rendering the father incompetent to help his son.

The Father agreed to come to therapy, and the therapist gave him the task to ask his son that night to be sure he kept his appointment in the schoolyard with the therapist.

The therapist gave the father his first task in helping his son, in an attempt to bring the father closer to the son. The father responded with self-assurance about his ability to mobilize Eddy.

At this point, the father took charge: "Well, it won't be necessary for you to meet him in school. I'll bring him to your office." Dr. P. V. said, "Thank you, Eduardo, you saved me a trip; I'll be ready for your family tomorrow at 6 P.M. Thanks again for all your help."

4/11/84

The whole family came in. After thanking both parents for helping the therapist bring the whole family together, the therapist turned to the father to ask him to introduce his children.

The therapist acknowledged the parent's competence in carrying out the task. The therapist placed the father in charge of the family (rather than in the disengaged position). As a way of consolidating the gains made in overcoming the mother's ambivalence toward bringing the whole family into therapy, the therapist placed the father in charge in the first session.

The girls were introduced first, then the father said, "Finally, this is Eddy, our son, and the one who's giving us such a hard time." Eddy bowed his head in pain at this comment. The therapist came closer to him and said, "I'm sorry that you were introduced in such a negative light, but perhaps *we* can just listen to your father's pain for you and put aside the angry tone."

The therapist as a joining tactic acknowledged Eddy's pain and then reframed the father's position (from rejecting to desperate). In addition, the therapist pointed out that Eddy and his father had something in common: They were both in pain. This helped to spread the IPhood and also set the stage for future work in developing a close relationship between them and lessened, to a degree, the estrangement they had been experiencing.

The therapist lifted Eddy's face to make him look directly at him and to help him reassume a head-erect position.

A bold maneuver to create closeness and move Eddy away from the "patient" role. Touching a 17-year-old male's face is risky in a first session. This therapist took the risk because Eddy came across as sensitive and dejected, and the therapist correctly assumed that Eddy would accept this move.

Eddy smiled, "Okay, so what do you want me to say?" Dr. P. V. answered, "Well, anything that you feel is important." Eddy began to cry and said, "I don't have any friends, and I only use drugs so that my friends will like me." Dr. P. V. responded, "Eddy, your father and I were once 17 years old, and we know how important it is for a young man to be liked by his friends. I know we can help you."

The therapist further strengthened his alliance with the father by referring to both himself and the father in terms of "we were 17 years old once." Moreover, the therapist attempted to bring father and son closer together as part of the same maneuver.

The first step in working with families in which one parent is distant is to ally the distant parent with the IP around issues related to the IP's problems. In this fashion, the enmeshed mother–son relationship is challenged.

The initial resistance was found in the mother's ambivalent behavior: The mother both wanted help and did not want the father involved in therapy. The resistance was overcome by tracking through the mother to the father directly and by placing the father more in charge of bringing the family into treatment, a strategy that was successful in overcoming the resistance to coming to treatment as a whole family.

CASE III: DISENGAGED PARENT

The Portillo Family

Identified Patient: Julio, age 15
      Stepfather: Victor, age 35
         Mother: Rosa, age 35
        Brother: Edgar, age 6

9/5/84

The mother called the clinic. She was referred to the clinic by the hospital where her son was being treated for an overdose the night before. The therapist gave her an appointment for the next day to immediately follow the son's release from the hospital at 11:00 A.M. The therapist explained that the stepfather must also come. The younger brother was left out, given the nature of the presenting problem and his tender age.

9/6/84

Rosa and Julio came to the appointment without the stepfather. When questioned, the mother stated that the father refused to come because he would be recorded on the records of a drug program, thereby jeopardizing his career. With the mother's permission, the therapist spent a few minutes reassuring the son of his willingness and ability to help him but explained that he would do best to spend the rest of their time contacting the stepfather directly, as his participation was essential.

> *In the office the therapist spent a long time establishing a therapeutic alliance with Rosa and Julio, reassuring them of his support in a manner that helped them to sense his expertise, ability, and concern. However, the therapist purposefully refused to initiate therapy without the father's being involved. To have done so would have been a reinforcement of a structural arrangement that kept the father distant and undervalued in his son's life.*
>
> *The initial diagnostic impression was that this could either be a case of a mother's ambivalence protecting the father's resistance, or else it could be a case of a disengaged father. While the mother's ambivalence was not clear, the therapist nevertheless decided to contact the father directly.*

Mother and son agreed to proceed this way. The therapist agreed to call back as soon as he had talked to the father. That afternoon the therapist reached the father at work. He refused to talk in depth to the therapist except to say, "You must work with my son individually; he's old enough." Assuming a puzzled attitude at his refusal to cooperate, the therapist confronted the father on the matter of his concern for a son who just almost killed himself. The father confessed his love for his boy but explained that the marriage to his wife was in a terrible state and that he believed their participation in therapy would be detrimental rather than helpful to his son. The attitude was one of "We can't even help each other, much less him. His mother has already hurt him enough; keep him away from her."

The alienation between the parents was most relevant, since their energies were being spent mostly in rejecting each other rather than helping the son. The father's anger toward the mother kept distance between the spouses and probably also kept the mother dependent on the son for emotional support. The father labeled the mother incompetent and in turn experienced his own incompetence in his inability to help his son. The parental conflict had created in the whole family a state of helplessness and hopelessness. The son's sacrificial creation of a crisis was a cry for help for both himself and the parents. This contact with the father clarified the diagnosis. The father was making every effort to maintain his distance from his wife and Julio. Hence, the resistance to entering treatment as a whole family was diagnosed as resulting from a disengaged parent.

The therapist empathized with the father's feelings of frustration and desperation, but added, "However, Victor, running away is never the solution. In a way that's what your son tried to do, and you see how destructive that can end up being, one way or another." The father said, "What do you expect me to do? This woman won't listen to anything I say. We always end up fighting." The therapist suggested, "Let me talk to your wife. I think I can get her to agree to put the differences between the two of you 'on hold' so we can all attend to Julio first."

The therapist had to begin to establish a sense of competence and hope in this family quickly, but he could not use the son, for he was already too overwhelmed by his sense of responsibility and centrality. The therapist had to thus move to ally strongly with the mother, giving her support and guidance in reaching her husband on behalf of their son.

9/6/84

The therapist called the mother after talking to the father and asked to meet her individually. She agreed to come to the clinic immediately. Once she was in the office, the therapist spent much time allowing the mother to ventilate her feelings of anger, frustration, and desperation. To each of her concerns the therapist replied, "I understand and I tell you we can work all this through if you and Victor agree to involve yourselves in therapy in a cooperative fashion, for Julio's sake."

The therapist began to hear the history of how after Julio's father died unexpectedly when the child was 2 years old, Rosa married Victor 2 years later. Ever since, Victor had been the only father that Julio had known. While she idealized her first marriage, the current marriage had soured after a few years. The therapist listened for clues of how this marriage had gone wrong. The main clue came in discovering that some years ago the husband began to do some heavy drinking after work and weekends, and his wife began to criticize him, belittling him and distancing him from her son. Although agreeing with the wife that the husband's problem drinking was totally undesirable, the therapist was able to convince the wife that the way in which she approached the problem was not effective. Rather, she had probably worsened the problem by making her husband feel rejected, disrespected, and alone.

The therapist joined the wife in the content of her complaint, but challenged her response, which had resulted in her rejecting and distancing her husband.

The therapist explained to the wife that despite her feelings of anger toward her husband, she must put her son's well-being ahead of her anger and become involved in therapy for two reasons: (1) Her son needed a father and might very well have done this as a desperate way of getting his parents together; (2) maybe this could eventually lead to her husband's working on his drinking, too.

In cases of disengaged parents, the resistance is overcome by giving the mother the task of getting closer to the father and by encouraging her in caring for the problems of their drug-abusing child. The IP becomes the content around which the mother approaches the father. Care is taken to insulate larger marital conflicts at this time until the family is engaged, at which time they can be addressed in therapy.

The therapist was successful in "selling" this idea to the mother, who confessed that despite her anger, she loved her husband and wanted to do whatever was needed for her son.

Very often in reframing a therapist has to be a good salesman. He must "sell" a new view, a new observation, a new alternative to the family, in order for them to be willing to risk change. He must do so from a position of close alliance in order to be successful. The new perspective the therapist "sells" to the family need not present accurately the total reality, but it does need to be strategically directed to mobilize new behaviors. In this case the new behaviors needed are those that would permit the family to come to therapy. The therapist was fully aware of the complex dynamic interactions of an alcoholic marriage, but such data was better used later on in therapy.

The therapist then directed the mother to prepare her husband's most favorite dinner for that evening and afterward to speak to him privately. In this private conversation she was to ask her husband, after confessing that she had not been supportive of him, to please put aside his anger and agree to work with her in helping their son. Most important was that she make him feel needed in a way that only he could fulfill.

The therapist set up a homework task that altered the interaction of Rosa and Victor from distance and war to cooperation and truce. This was done "on behalf of Julio."

To Rosa's protestations that "it's too late for that," the therapist simply replied, "You are doing this for Julio; it cannot be too late for Julio." To instill confidence in her ability to soften the tension with her husband, the therapist, who was a male, said, "You women have a special way of making us guys forget the negative. All you have to do is show us that you love us, and we're right back in. And Rosa, we only need for Victor to be back in as far as having hope and wanting to cooperate. If you can get him to that place, I'll take over from there as a therapist." Rosa agreed to put on all her charm and "deliver."

If the mother could move her husband to therapy, hope would be instilled by their being successful, and the husband and wife would be engaged in a task that would bring them to mutual cooperation—saving their son. Later on, after Julio was doing well, this same alliance between husband and wife, an alliance that would allow them to experience their ability to be competent, would enable the couple to work together on their marital issues.

9/7/84

The wife called the clinic. She carried out her task. Despite her husband's initial reluctance and aggressiveness, strengthened by the therapist's strong support she persisted and was able to convince him to come to therapy. The therapist congratulated her and set up an appointment for the whole family. To reinforce the wife's work, the therapist asked her permission to call her husband directly and echo her statements to him about how important and central the father's help was in treating the son, as well as about how caring a father he was, to put aside his marital issues to come forth for his son.

The therapist set up a task that moved the parents from disengagement to union; the goal was helping the son. The change was a structural one that realigned the system in a manner that brought the parents together, allowing the whole family to come into therapy.

9/8/84
The family showed up for intake and the first session.

CASE IV: THERAPY AS AN EXPOSÉ

The Soto Family

Identified Patient: Lourdes, age 14
Father: Carlos, age 34
Mother: Cristina, age 33
Brother: Hector, age 12

1/12/84
The mother called the clinic most worried about her daugher, who together with her boyfriend had a group of drug-involved friends. They were also involved in school truancy together. The mother stated she was very afraid because the father had said that either this ends or he would beat up the boyfriend and put an end to this in "his way." The therapist listened intently to the mother's fears and empathized whole-heartedly, reiterating that the matter needed to be attended to before something ugly happened. Cristina was given an appointment and told that of course the whole family needed to come in, since everyone's feelings and reactions were involved in the problem.

> *The therapist's patience, listening skills, and empathetic warmth were used immediately to begin developing a "joined" position, which was the foundation of the therapeutic system.*

1/13/84
Cristina called back, stating that her husband refused to come to the clinic. When her daughter heard this, she said she wasn't coming either. The therapist asked for her husband's number at work so he could speak to him directly. The mother agreed.

The therapist called the father, who was initially angry about being bothered at work. The therapist apologized, explaining that he too hated to do this, but he had heard from the mother how the girl's situation was so critical that "we should do something now before things get worse." The father agreed about the critical nature, and the therapist continued to listen, concerned and empathic to "how bad these kids today are getting. One cannot be too careful."

The therapist joined the father in a "buddy-buddy" talk about the hardships of raising a kid nowadays, and through this alliance got the father to confide in him.

As a result of this "man-to-man" talk, the father began to relax and eventually explained to the therapist that he did not want to come to therapy because he had had a mistress for some time now. Although the family knew about it, "things have been left alone." He was afraid that in therapy this would come up and worried that "all sorts of feelings are going to be let loose." The therapist acknowledged his understanding of the sensitivity of the situation and added, "However there are ways in which we can all agree to attend solely to your concerns as parents for Lourdes and leave adult matters aside. As a matter of fact, I can see to it that such discussions are not entered into, because in reality those things need to be dealt with apart from the children. That is, if you ever decide to deal with it at all." The therapist then suggested that he talk to Cristina and, if it was okay with the father, he would have Cristina be the one who made Lourdes come to therapy. The father agreed, with the admonition, "If Cristina gets on my case, I'm out," to which the therapist replied, "I'll see to it that we just concentrate on Lourdes."

The therapist needed to present to the family a new view of therapy that permitted the daughter's problem to be dealt with while still giving the family, at least initially, the alternative to continue the conspiracy of silence about the infidelity. In reality the youngster might have been engaging in attention-getting behavior as a provocation to get father's attention. She might also have been acting out the mother's anger. If this provocation went unattended, she might well need to "up the ante."

The therapist agreed with the father, as a compromise to engage him in therapy, that the father would become involved as long as his personal life was not brought into the therapy. This was a strategic maneuver on the part of the therapist that later might be challenged.

1/13/84

The therapist called the mother and assured her that the father would be coming if he was made to feel comfortable about the therapy contract, so it was up to the mother to convince her daughter to come. This was a difficult job because in some ways what her daughter wanted was just the opposite of what the father wanted. The therapist added, "It is important, Cristina, that you follow my instructions to the letter." "Agreed, agreed," said Cristina.

The therapist commissioned the mother to reassure the father that the clinic would only be interested in the daughter's problems with school and behavior, while reassuring the daughter that the clinic was interested in helping not just her but the whole family to get along better. The mother, of course, was to speak to the father and the daughter separately. Since the family was expert in keeping secrets, the mother was told to ask both to keep their thoughts and plans about coming to themselves until the first visit.

> *This was a family that was keeping a secret. The daughter, like everyone else, knew about the secret and was angry that she was being scapegoated when there were others in the family who were also "misbehaving." Very often families deal with a serious conflict by denying it and detouring it in another direction. To deny a conflict is to pretend it doesn't exist. To detour it is to place its energies and feelings, even the burden of its resolution, into another conflict that is exaggerated, mishandled, or created. Notice the use of mimesis in giving a task that involved keeping secrets.*

1/14/86

The family came to see the therapist. The therapist took great care to join each member individually in order to make each feel supported. The therapist made sure to act nonjudgmentally toward all and rejected all attempts made to get him to take sides. He repeatedly returned to the view, "There are no good and bad guys in families, just people struggling in life who sometimes have difficulty dealing with each other."

The therapist then presented to the family four alternatives: (1) the father could eventually (very soon) have his threatened fight with the boyfriend and risk potential and probably serious trouble for all. "This sort of trouble has a way of going in uncontrolled directions." (2) The family could come to therapy to deal only with the issue of "how to help the daughter to make better decisions on her own behalf, so that she will gain successful independence." Any other issues could be contracted to be left out of the therapy session in deference to the daughter's emergency, thus obviating any possible excuses to avoid therapy. (3) The family could come to therapy to deal with all the issues that were affecting it, if the members felt so moved and ready. The therapist reassured the family of his expertise and experience in dealing with such situations many times prior, thus increasing their sense of confidence in the therapeutic system. (4) The family could negotiate therapy only for the daughter's problem now and agree to renegotiate in the future, when the daughter is fine, whether to continue therapy to move into the other issues or to leave it at that. The therapist wrote all four alternatives on the blackboard and gave the family members the task of discussing them among themselves and announcing their joint decision.

The therapist asked the family to discuss these four alternatives fully and planned to ally with the daughter to manipulate her into taking the fourth position so that the family would be engaged, the daughter would be removed from the position of IP, and the family would feel assured that it had an option later on to open up or not. By resolving this first task together, they began to experience cooperation and competence in achieving success.

Meanwhile, the therapist sat close to the daughter and coached her to assume the position of alternative 4. "After all, Lourdes, there are other problems in this family, and if they don't get together in helping you first, you'll continue to be their scapegoat and all their other frustrations will be inadvertently taken out on you."

With the therapist's alliance, the daughter convinced the family to opt for option 4 and agreed to start therapy.

The therapist made their first appointment, commenting, "You see, today you already resolved what seemed like an impossible conflict, and you did it quite effectively and jointly. You're already well on your way."

The therapist supported the daughter in advocating for choice 4. The family opted for this choice and agreed to start therapy.

Unlike traditional intrapersonal therapy, this approach is strategic in that it is specifically formulated to deal with the family's first presenting problem, that is, resistance to treatment. It is not intended to be a search for truth or justice. The therapist had used the mother's motivation and the daughter's ingenious acting out to bring the family to therapy. He then reframed the family's view of therapy: from a place where all is exposed without choice or control to one where people have options about what to work on at what acceptable pace.

Part V

Working with One Person

Throughout this book our aim has been to look to the family for help when one of its members signals for help. What sets us apart as family therapists is that we wish to maintain the integrity and interdependence of the family members. This usually means involving the entire family, whenever possible, in the therapeutic process.

In spite of our best efforts, there are instances in which it is not possible to work with the whole family for the full treatment program. What is a family therapist to do?

Are there ways of fulfilling our commitment to family change even when we have access to only one troubled family member? The next chapter explores this quandary.

To meet the challenge presented by a problem as recalcitrant and resistant to change as drug abuse, we have found that we have had to go beyond even some of the most basic assumptions of conventional family therapy. Conventional family therapy as usually implemented is based on the assumption that it is necessary to have the entire family present in order to bring about change in family structure. Although it is certainly desirable to have the entire family present, it is sometimes impractical or impossible for a therapist to engage an entire family. In such cases it is necessary to go beyond even the most basic assumptions of conventional family therapy. Part V of this book provides the reader with the knowledge and understanding of a set of tools, rooted in structural techniques, that are designed to accomplish the goals of family therapy while working primarily with only one family member. This set of strategies is integrated into a therapeutic model that we call *One Person Family Therapy*. It attempts to go beyond the conventional strategies of family therapy, in that it makes available family-oriented techniques that have proven to be effective in treating drug abuse in cases where it is impractical to work with entire families.

8

One Person Family Therapy

A 17-year-old woman, Silvia, was referred by a probation officer for a minor legal infraction. She had left home, stopped going to school, and was living with a 22-year-old intravenous drug user. Her family was in turmoil. Emotions such as anger, guilt, pity, hopelessness, and despair were rampant; communication lines had collapsed. The father, when contacted, identified the daughter as the source of the family's problems and stated that he did not care to be helpful to his daughter "the tramp," much less to be involved in treatment.

The family therapist assumes that although the problem adolescent is the one displaying a whole host of behavior problem symptoms, the entire family is in some way involved in maintaining these problems. Thus although the youth is the IP, the therapist recognizes that the family's patterns of interaction are maladaptive.

Logically, since the entire family is involved in the problem, the therapist wishes to see the entire family together in therapy. However, this is not always possible. This may be because the IP is physically separated from the family, the family is unusually strong in its belief that the IP is the only one who needs to be cured, or the identified patient insists on being seen alone. In the case of Silvia the therapist recognized that this was a particularly difficult family therapy challenge because all three of these reasons existed.

This chapter addresses the issue of how to handle this situation: A client/family appears to need the benefit of family therapy but circumstances make seeing the whole family during most therapy sessions impractical or impossible. In this chapter we will describe the techniques we have developed for doing One Person Family Therapy. One Person Family Therapy is *designed to accomplish the goals of family therapy while working primarily with only one family member.*

A therapist using One Person Family Therapy (OPFT) techniques tries to achieve the same two goals of *conjoint* family therapy (i.e., family therapy with the entire family present). First, the therapist works to change the way family members act toward each other so that they will not do or say things that might unwittingly contribute to maintaining or promoting the IP's symptoms. Second, the therapist works to reduce the symptoms exhibited by the IP—that is, to reduce or eliminate problem behaviors. To make the changes necessary to achieve these goals, the therapist will use the joining, diagnosing, and restructuring techniques described throughout this book. These techniques, however, have been modified for carrying out family therapy through one person, whom we will call the OP (i.e., "One Person" in therapy). The OP, we would point out, is usually also the IP, but we have changed the term in this case from IP to OP in order to highlight the reason we work with this person alone is *not* because she or he is the only one in need, but rather as a strategic maneuver through which we will gain access to the entire family process. Through this OP we will seek to change the family's maladaptive patterns of interaction. The next sections explain how to modify our usual structural family therapy techniques of joining, diagnosing, and restructuring for use in One Person Family Therapy.

JOINING

As in conjoint family therapy, the initial objective is to join the family. In OPFT, since the entire family is not available for most or all treatment sessions, the therapist must enter the family, as well as direct change, through the OP. The first step in accomplishing this is to establish a therapeutic alliance with the OP. That is, the therapist must create a close working relationship of trust and goodwill with the OP. The therapist must demonstrate to the OP that she or he is sensitive to the OP's needs and values and sufficiently skilled to help solve the OP's problems.

In the case of Silvia the therapist began the joining process in the first session by establishing a therapeutic alliance. Silvia presented herself for the first session in a punkish, revealing outfit and gave the impression of being a tough adolescent who took pride in flaunting her streetwise experiences. She was initially distant and caustic to the therapist. The therapist opened by empathizing with Silvia's almost certain dislike for the probation officer who sent her to therapy. This opening encouraged Silvia to express her disgust with the probation officer and with therapy. Having gotten this out of the way, she recounted enthusiastically her worldly experiences after having moved out of her parents' home. This situation provided the opportunity for the therapist to establish rapport and create a therapeutic alliance. The therapist, sensing Silvia's great pride in her adventure as a woman of the world, listened intently and allowed Silvia to savor her bold adventure. (This is an example of what we earlier called maintenance, i.e., supporting a behavior for the sake of establishing rapport, even if we do not agree with the behavior.) By listening attentively the therapist and patient shared a critical experience and established a therapeutic alliance that provided a foundation from which to begin to assess the family structure and the position of Silvia within it.

DIAGNOSIS

In OPFT, as in engagement, because by definition the whole family is not present, it is not possible to administer the Family Tasks. Thus the therapist works with limited information to diagnose patterns of interactions that are supporting the symptoms. In order to identify the relevant maladaptive patterns, it becomes necessary to use a modification of the informal diagnosis that allows us to collect assessment information in other ways. In particular, it is the concept of an *enactment analogue* used in combination with the principle of complementarity that enables us to conduct an informal assessment of family interaction through only one person.

Whereas in conjoint family therapy informal assessments can be conducted on actual enactments elicited from the conjoint family by the Family Tasks, in OPFT, since just one person is present, only an "enactment analogue" is possible. The enactment analogue, as used in OPFT, refers to depicting through the OP's perceptions the family's characteristic interactional patterns, in lieu of actual direct observation.

Since we all tend to see what others do rather than our own behavior, when the OP is asked to represent her family, what she usually represents is her perception of the behavior of others rather than her own behaviors. The therapist assumes from systems theory that for the system to maintain itself, the OP must behave in a fashion that comple-

ments the reported behavior of others, that is, that the OP has interjected the kinds of behaviors that mesh with the behavior of others in
the family. The enactment analogue provides the opportunity to recon-
struct through inference the kinds of interactions that may occur in the
family by making use of the concept of complementarity.

The family interactional patterns are defined as comprising two
complementary parts: (1) the OP's own behavior in the family context,
and (2) the rest of the family's behavior. Because the OP tends to
perceive the other family members' behaviors but not her own, in the
enactment analogue the OP is requested to represent what she is aware
of, that is, the other family members' behaviors. The therapist learns
what the OP perceives other family members as doing. Then the
therapist assumes that the OP's behavior must be the complement of
what others are perceived as doing. Bringing together the family's
represented behaviors and the OP's assumed behaviors provides a full
picture of the family's systemic, self-reinforcing, and repetitive patterns
of interactions. This process is illustrated in the diagram contained in
Figure 8.1.

The therapist typically begins the enactment analogue by asking the
OP to describe or act out interactions between herself and other family
members. Usually the OP will say things like "Dad called me a whore,"
"Grandma yelled," and so on. That is, the OP tends to perceive that
everyone is down on her. In the case of Silvia, when the therapist
inquired about her perception of the problem in the family, Silvia
responded by complaining that her family was a bore; they weren't
"with it." She stated that she had left home because she couldn't stand it
anymore. "I felt trapped. I wanted to have fun, to be free, to do my own
thing."

The therapist's goal is to get as complete a picture as possible and
then to fill in the missing information using his or her understanding of
complementarity. The process is somewhat like putting together a
jigsaw puzzle that has some missing pieces. The OP provides some of
the pieces. The therapist must then construct the missing pieces that
will fit with the pieces provided by the OP. These missing pieces are the
complements to the interactions as described by the OP. Once the
therapist has all the pieces, both the ones that had to be constructed and
the ones provided by the OP, she or he can put together the entire
puzzle and have a clear picture of the family's structure.

Asking for descriptions of what happens in the family is a strategy
borrowed directly from eliciting enactments in conjoint family therapy.
However, in working with one person it is helpful to use additional
strategies in identifying the family's patterns of interactions. One such
strategy is the *role play*. In role play the OP enacts some of the

FIGURE 8.1 Venn Diagrams of Family Interactions

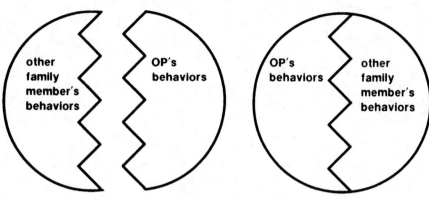

1. OP represents other family member's behavior.

2. Therapist assumes that family is a system and thus OP's behaviors must be the complement of what she or he has represented as behaviors of others.

3. Therapist constructs a symbolic representation of the family system/interactional patterns by bringing together the two complements (adds 1 and 2).

interactions and situations that occur within the family. The OP pretends to be someone other than herself and acts as this person would in a given situation.

In the case of Silvia, her relationship with her drug-dealing boyfriend provided the opportunity for playing the role of not only her father and mother, but her boyfriend as well. Silvia's role playing revealed that she perceived her boyfriend to be somewhat like her father: seductive and self-righteous. Her mother, on the other hand, was role played as a somewhat innocent person who saw no evil. Thus, for example, when the father engaged in "playful" but sexually suggestive behavior, the mother always came up with some cliché such as, "Silvia, you'll always be your daddy's and my little girl." Hence the mother at once encouraged Silvia to sit on her father's lap and failed to see the sexual undertones of the behavior. The father was portrayed as cloaking his jealousy of her boyfriends in self-righteousness. "He always yelled when I brought my boyfriends around: 'You're a tramp.'" The boyfriend was portrayed as being jealous of all of her friends. "He always gets angry when my friends come around." Both father and boyfriend were perceived as attempting to stifle Silvia's relationships with others.

During role playing the therapist often helps the OP recall incidents and relive them with almost the same emotional intensity as when they originally occurred. Or, he or she may help the OP devise situations that did not happen but could occur, as a way of exploring how a particular person in the family would handle a situation. Often the OP learns how she or he may act in an imaginary situation.

Often the therapist and OP engage in role play together. Here the therapist has a good opportunity to present various facets of family interactions, thus allowing the OP to see herself from several dimensions. This technique also enables the therapist to probe into areas the OP may possibly not delve into by herself. Thus the therapist is very active: an actor when engaging in role play, a director in encouraging the OP to assume the roles of family members, and, sometimes, a choreographer in physically rearranging seating patterns.

With the information on how the OP perceives significant others, the therapist explores the OP's complementary role that makes it possible for significant others to behave the way they do. This may be accomplished by asking questions such as "What do you do when your father asks you to sit on his lap?" "Are there special things that you do when you want to get something from your father?" "What are those things?" "Do you dress or act special for him?" "When did your father start calling you a tramp? Was there something that led up to it?" "Tell me about what happens between you and your boyfriend when your friends come over."

Combining the information from the enactment analogue, the role plays, and the OP's complementary behaviors, the therapist—working through the one person—uses an informal assessment strategy to arrive at a diagnosis of the maladaptive family interactions.

In the case of Silvia, father and daughter were enmeshed (loss of physical distance is evident), and mother was disengaged from both of them. The father-daughter relationship was conflictual, with the conflict having become overt when Silvia began to rebel against the closeness with her father and expressed her independence maladaptively by becoming pregnant at age 15. An important aspect of the conflict was around developmental stage, with the father attempting to maintain Silvia as his little girl and Silvia reacting by going to the other extreme of becoming a woman of the world.

RESTRUCTURING

Most therapists who do individual therapy try to change something inside their clients. Many therapists try to change their client's attitudes, thoughts, or personality. This type of change inside the person's mind we call *intrapersonal* change. Structural family therapists, on the other hand, try to change the way one person behaves toward another person. This type of change we call *interpersonal* change.

In OPFT the therapist sees only one person in most therapy sessions but tries to make changes in the entire family's structure. In order to accomplish this, the therapist must make both intra- and inter-personal changes. The strategy is to first make the intrapersonal changes in the OP seen in therapy, then use the OP as an ally to make interpersonal changes in the family. Sometimes the therapist will make all the necessary intrapersonal changes, then make all the interpersonal changes. Usually, however, it is more effective to select one facet of one problem (e.g., the sexualized relation between Silvia and her father), do all the necessary intrapersonal and interpersonal work on that one facet, and then move on to another facet. This type of progression, dealing with one thing at a time, usually seems to work best. This is not very different from the rule given by efficiency experts which states that one should do a task and complete it before going on to the next task.

Restructuring: Intrapersonal

During intrapersonal restructuring the therapist facilitates changes within the OP that are likely to promote changes in family structure. The therapist engages the OP by clarifying what it is that the OP wants and how certain family interactions may be interfering with the OP's achieving those goals. Once these undesirable/maladaptive interactions are identified, the therapist points out how the OP may be contributing to maintaining these interactions. Techniques that can be used to achieve the necessary intrapersonal restructuring are described next.

Diagraming the Family

Drawing a diagram of the interaction patterns, including the power hierarchy in the family, can clarify some of the role relationships that are hard for the OP to understand. Mapping the family's structure—as in the case of Frank in the next chapter—can be a useful tool in facilitating restructuring.

Role Play

Role play, in addition to being helpful for eliciting enactment analogues, is also useful in intrapersonal restructuring. By having the OP take on the role of various significant others, she can learn to better empathize with them as well as gain a greater understanding of how they perceive her and her behavior. Further, the OP is able to verbalize within the safe environment of the therapist's office feelings and fears that may have been unspoken in her actual relation to these significant others. This technique is effective as a rehearsal for a later encounter with that person. For example, the therapist had identified Silvia's older sister as a potentially stabilizing force for Silvia and thus sought to explore ways of bringing Silvia and her sister closer together. In exploring this relationship Silvia expressed that she would like to tell her older sister how much she admires her and wants to be her friend. However, since early childhood she has felt threatened by her and afraid to reveal her feelings. When the therapist assigns to Silvia the task of opening up to her sister, it will be easier to carry out this difficult assignment after having role played it during the session. Thus the therapist had Silvia role play opening up to her sister as well as role play her sister's response to her, processing Silvia's fears and apprehensions as they arose.

Reframing

In all families, members have a certain impression of each other. This tends to color the way they regard and behave toward each other. For example, in problem families the negative aspects of some individual are highlighted and the positive qualities of others are also exaggerated. In these cases it is always useful early in therapy to reframe the perception that all of the family's problems are due to one individual's misbehavior. This can be done by spreading the IPhood around. In intrapersonal restructuring during OPFT, the process of spreading the IPhood around necessarily begins with the OP. Reframing begins by changing the OP's perception that she is the family's repository for blame. In reframing the therapist seeks to help the OP or other family members to see their own and others' situations in a new light, a different way of viewing the underlying meaning of behavior and communication. In Silvia's case the therapist sought to reframe Silvia's relationship with her father in interactive terms: her father, while calling her a tramp, clearly encouraged her to flirt with him. Hence he encouraged the behavior that he criticized. In addition to spreading the IPhood around her "tramp behavior," this intervention served to create distance between father and daughter, thereby moderating the enmeshment.

Increasing Stress and Provoking Crises

These are related techniques that are used to help motivate or mobilize a person or family to change. It is very difficult to change people if they do not believe that anything is wrong. Raising an individual's stress level or provoking a crisis makes that person acutely aware of the need for change. This technique is often needed if the family tends to deny or avoid problems. In actual practice there are a variety of ways to apply these techniques. In general, the therapist can emphasize or exaggerate some aspect of an issue, can needle some family members, or can temporarily side with one family member against other family members.

While one of the family's issues with Silvia was her relationship with a no good bum/intravenous drug user, and thus a structural issue, it was possible to intervene in that relationship by creating a crisis around a specific *content*. Thus, for example, the therapist worked at some length to bring Silvia to awareness and a sense of crisis about her sexual relationship with her boyfriend, because of the danger of AIDS. Whereas this content in itself is clearly important, the therapist used the content to attempt to create a structural change that would increase the distance between Silvia and her boyfriend.

Splitting the OP's Executive Observant Ego

In this technique, after the OP has described an event, the therapist asks the OP to objectively observe the OP in the scene. The OP presents a scenario that both, therapist and OP, watch together. The OP describes an imaginary scene depicting a family interaction in which the OP is involved. Thus the OP has two roles: One role is as the OP engaging in interaction and conflict with the members of her family; the other is as an observer objectively watching the conflict along with the therapist, as if it were a movie on television. In this activity the role of the therapist is to help the OP to objectively observe and interpret her or his behavior. More specifically, the therapist will show the OP how she or he has contributed to the interactions that caused the OP to be singled out as the family scapegoat, helping the OP to understand the OP's complementary role in the family structure.

The OP learns how she or he has participated in accepting the role she is in. In that way, the OP can take responsibility for problem behavior that is a reaction to how someone in the family is behaving toward the OP. Further, she or he learns to reframe her self-perception from "I am a problem person" to "I am behaving in such a way that it is placing me in a role that creates problems for me."

In Silvia's case this technique allowed her to "observe" the interactional sequence in which she was involved. The therapist asked Silvia to imagine seeing herself in the family context while the interaction was ongoing. Thus Silvia was "asked to observe along with the therapist" an imagined family interaction. The part of Silvia that observed the interaction was her executive observant ego. The other part of Silvia was the part imagined to be participating in the interaction, that is, the Silvia playing the IP role that complemented the rest of the family system. As

Silvia observed the imagined family interactions, she was taught by the therapist how she contributed to those interactions and how she contributed to being labeled the identified patient through her precocious sexual behaviors.

Restructuring: Interpersonal

When the OP has established a therapeutic alliance with the therapist, is beginning to understand her complementary role in the family, and is ready to relinquish that role, it is time to begin restructuring the family. In family therapy when the entire family is present, restructuring takes place directly through therapist interventions that change family interactions as they occur during a therapy session. In OPFT the therapist creates changes in family interactions by changing those OP behaviors that help to maintain the maladaptive interactions. The OP, as an agent of the therapist, goes home to bring about changes in the family. As this happens the therapist will make full use of the principle of complementarity. The therapist must plan his or her strategy carefully to make the most effective use of the family members' complementary role relationships with the OP. The family structure is changed when the OP changes the way she behaves and the other family members adjust to the changes in the OP. Several useful restructuring techniques are described below.

Task Setting

As discussed in the engagement chapter, tasks are an essential tool for working outside the therapy session. In OPFT tasks are planned in collaboration with the OP. As usual, the purpose of the tasks is to alter ways the family has interacted for many years. The other family members, therefore, will be resistant to change. The only way to overcome this resistance is for the OP to be very confident of what she is doing. Rehearsals through role playing are the best way to achieve this confidence.

Tasks should focus on interactions between family members rather than on what the individual can do by herself. At the beginning, tasks should be easy to accomplish so that they can provide successful experiences. An early difficult or failed task may prove to be too discouraging and may even cause the OP and/or the family to withdraw from therapy.

Reversals

With this maneuver the therapist attempts to change rigid and maladaptive patterns of behavior. In reversals the therapist suggests the OP do something that is the opposite or very different from the OP's usual behavior. For example, if the OP rarely communicates with her sister, the therapist suggests that she talk to her sister about a recent experience. Since this relationship has a history of estrangement, this act can provide a breakthrough and an opening for a new behavior. Reversals are useful in creating the opportunity for new interactional patterns to emerge. In Silvia's case, for example, the therapist coached Silvia to set limits on her father when he was flirtatious and to stand up to him when he denigrated her. System change takes place because when Silvia changes her behavior, in effect she has interrupted the flow of the family interactions that cast her into the IP role. This is a clear example of how OPFT differs from many other psychotherapies that focus on intrapersonal change only. It does not stop at creating awareness. Instead it uses awareness as a tool for redirecting the interpersonal behavior of the OP, thereby bringing about change in the family.

In conjoint family therapy the therapist can cause this interruption of the maladaptive family interactions during family sessions, because the therapist is present to promote the change. In OPFT, however, the therapist must rely heavily on the OP's ability to change her or his own behavior and to maintain the change in the face of strong family pressure to return to the family's old, habitual pattern of interactions. Hence in using OPFT the therapist must rehearse with the OP her change in behavior. It is particularly important to role play various alternative outcomes that can ensue from the OP's change. The purpose of the rehearsal is to allow the therapist to overcome any resistance in the OP, to give the OP an experience of mastery, and to attempt to prevent possible family sabotage of the OP's new behaviors.

Detriangulation

Often when two family members have a conflict that goes unresolved, they will involve a third party. This triangulation is usually very destructive. In OPFT there are recommended ways for working with triangles, certain strategies that are employed in conjoint therapy must be avoided. In every instance the therapist must avoid giving tasks to the OP that involve attempting to handle a conflict between two other people, particularly when the two other people are the parents. Whereas in conjoint family therapy the therapist intervenes directly to highlight the marital conflict, in OPFT the OP can only intervene to break up the triangle by creating distance between the OP and the marital conflict. Thus, for example, in the case of Silvia it would not have been advisable for Silvia to attempt to address the disengagement between her mother and father because such an intervention on her part would have further triangulated her. Rather, in response to conflict (covert as it was on the part of Silvia's parents) the appropriate and adaptive behavior for Silvia was for her to "walk away" or remove herself from the scene of the conflict.

In summary, to achieve the goals of OPFT, the therapist must strategically restructure both intrapersonally with the OP and interpersonally in the family, using the OP as a therapeutic ally. When restructuring *intra*personally, the therapist prepares the OP to make the necessary changes in the family structure. Generally this means helping the OP to (1) decide what the OP wants and needs, and (2) understand the OP's complementary roles in the family and how the OP contributes to family interactions.

Building on the intrapersonal restructuring, it is possible to work with the OP to change those parts of the family's structure that maintain or contribute to the OP's problem behaviors. This is called *inter*personal restructuring. In order to accomplish these changes, interactions with two characteristics are strategically chosen: (1) They are maladaptive, and (2) they are ones in which the OP plays an important role. Maladaptive interactions are selected for intervention because ours is a problem-focused approach that targets maladaptive interactions. Interactions in which the OP plays an important role are chosen because, according to the principle of complementarity, the OP can only restructure interactions by changing her or his behavior in those interactions in which the OP is involved. If the OP changes her or his behavior in interactions in which the OP plays an important role, the concept of complementarity predicts that the others involved in the interaction must also change in order to accommodate the new behavior (that is, if the OP's behavior changes, the behavior of the other people involved must also change in order to mesh and coordinate with the change). This complementary change cannot occur if the OP is not already involved in an interaction. The only way to make changes in interactions in which the OP is not involved is if the rest of the family is available to come in for some therapy sessions.

In the best of all worlds, when the OP changes, the family will accommodate itself to the change, thereby reinforcing the new behavior. However, in the real world the response to the OP's changed behavior is family pressure to return to its previous patterns of interactions. The confrontation between the OP's trying to create change and the family's trying to prevent it will tend to produce a family crisis. At this point families are often accessible to the therapist. Thus it is an ideal moment for the therapist to request and typically obtain a family therapy session.

A family session or two also provides an opportunity—albeit a limited one—for the therapist to intervene directly in family interac-

tional patterns in which the OP cannot intervene or does not participate. However, it may not be possible in one or two family sessions to
bring about major structural changes in these other maladaptive patterns. Rather, it is only possible to change those aspects of these "other"
maladaptive interactions as they affect the OP. Thus in the case of Silvia
the therapist might have worked with Silvia's mother to encourage her
to set limits on the father's sexually suggestive behavior toward Silvia.
While the therapist might not have addressed the larger difficulty that
Silvia's mother had in being assertive with the father, the therapist
targeted promoting assertiveness in the mother in the circumscribed
area of sexually suggestive behaviors toward Silvia.

9

One Person Family Therapy: The Alfaro Family

*José Szapocznik, Franklin H. Foote,
Angel Perez-Vidal, Olga Hervis,
and William M. Kurtines*

In order to give the reader an overall feel for the OPFT approach, a full case is summarized below.

BACKGROUND

Frank was a 19-year-old Cuban American who was both working and attending community college. He was the IP and became the OP for

The work presented in this chapter was funded by National Institute on Drug Abuse Grant No. 5R18 DA0322 01-03. The case history in this chapter is based on an actual case seen by Dr. Angel Perez-Vidal.

therapy. His family complained about his extensive use of marijuana and occasional cocaine use and, since he worked with his father, was afraid that the drug abuse would not only be detrimental to Frank but also eventually compromise his father's position at work. Frank was frustrated, angry, and at the point of "giving up" completely. He felt he had disillusioned everyone in the family and was the family's only "sore spot." Further, he felt guilty that his parents were arguing over him constantly. He had practically no relationship with his sister Elsa, a 16-year-old high school senior. He felt she was always doing everything right, while he was always "the black sheep" of the family.

Not only did other family members view Frank as the IP, but he also viewed himself as the IP, that is, as being the cause of all troubles in the family. Thus he himself contributed to the maintenance of his own IPhood. This situation exacerbated his feelings of inadequacy and per-petuated his dependency on his parents.

Elsa, age 16, was doing very well in school and had a normal social life. She had a good relationship with both parents, though she was not very close to either. Although she had experimented with pot on a couple of occasions, she had decided it was not for her. Her circle of friends was also not drug involved.

The opposite of Frank's IPhood, Elsa was perceived to be the reposi-tory of psychological health in this family. Her behavior and attitude both within the family and in the world outside were adequate and successful.

Hilda, age 42, was the mother of Frank and Elsa. For most of her life she had been a housewife, although recently she had been asking to be allowed to study and work outside of the home. She had overprotected her son, to the point of covering up his drug use even to her husband. By the start of therapy she felt overwhelmed and tried to blame her husband and son for all the problems around her. Although the marital relationship was deteriorating, the conflict between husband and wife manifested itself around only two issues: parenting Frank and the father's refusal to let Hilda work.

Hilda's overly protective and overly involved dyadic interaction with Frank clearly had prevented him from achieving a healthy separation from the family at the time of his adolescent development. This type of relationship contributed to Frank's drug abuse. His dependence on her was reinforced by her covering up his drug abuse. This cover-up is also an indication that this family could not confront problems directly and honestly. Instead, conflict avoidance and denial were used as protective devices. Frank's drug use, for example, was serving to detour conflict in the spousal system.

Mario, 44 years old, was the father of Frank and Elsa. Although he was a high school drop out, he had worked successfully as an automotive parts salesman since arriving in the United States 20 years ago and had been able to provide a lower-middle class level of income for the family. He criticized his son and wife severely for their failures and inefficiencies. He considered the "whole thing" as a personal affront and was very aggressive and hostile. He had gotten a job for Frank in the company where he worked, to "keep an eye on him while trying to make something out of him." He blamed his wife for Frank's problems.

Mario's lack of empathy and understanding of his son and wife contributed to forcing them into a strong alliance with each other.

Summary of Sessions

Session 1 (Conjoint Session)

Mrs. A. called the clinic to set an appointment, having been referred by a friend who was an ex-client. Mrs. A. told the therapist that her son refused to come in for therapy. The therapist insisted on talking to the son on the phone and convinced him that he wanted to help the whole family, not blame him further. The therapist explained further that he felt Frank needed some help in dealing with his family and getting pressure "off his back" so he could feel better. Frank agreed to come. An appointment was set for the next day for an initial session and the administration of the Family Tasks.

The therapists tracked from mother to Frank in order to join very early in the therapeutic process. The therapist immediately engaged and allied with Frank by making use of Frank's own concerns: the way the family perceived and treated him.

Making an immediate appointment capitalized on the family's sense of urgency. An additional clear message was given: that the therapist felt the problem was important and that he wanted to help.

Even in OPFT, having the initial session include the entire family facilitates the therapist's job and speeds up the therapeutic process. It does so by allowing the therapist to administer the Family Tasks and observe the family's interactions directly. It also gives him the opportunity to join the whole family in a therapeutic alliance to ease the tension surrounding Frank's well-being.

The Family Tasks revealed an alliance between the mother and Frank, a peripheral father, the strong IPhood of Frank, and attempts at conflict avoidance and denial. Frank was triangulated in the spousal conflict. For a 19-year-old, Frank was highly dependent on his parents and his mother was highly overprotective, indicating that the family was functioning at a lower developmental level than would be appropriate for a 19-year-old.

As will be seen, the Alfaro family is a case example in which a combination of one person and conjoint techniques were used. After the initial conjoint session, the first major effort of the therapist was targeted at the problems around developmental stage. For this reason, the next several sessions used OPFT techniques in working with Frank to help him individuate and separate from the family. As noted, while encouraging a more healthy degree of separation for Frank, the therapist was at the same time protective of the integrity of the family system.

Before the family came in the therapist arranged chairs in a circle. As they came in, they sat in the following order: father, mother, sister, and IP. Initially the therapist sat next to the father.

A circle can be very conducive to communication. Family members and the therapist can watch one another's faces as they speak to each other. It also makes the therapist physically part of the group.

BSFT therapists often are able to find important clues from seating patterns. In this case, the therapist immediately noticed that father and son sat on opposite ends of the family, leaving a break between father and son. In most Cuban American families the father is the head of the power hierarchy, at least nominally. Therefore the therapist chose to sit next to the father as an initial step toward entering the family system through the main power figure in the family, the father. Later in the session he shifted chairs to be next to Frank, in order to ally with him and lend him greater power in the therapeutic system.

Mario immediately began to take over, complaining and criticizing Frank, pointing to his son's failures, and adding some comments questioning Hilda's parenting of Frank. The complaints about Frank centered around his drug use: He was good for nothing; he was about to lose his job; he embarrassed his father; he was always late.

Quickly Hilda joined in the barrage of criticism, supporting what Mario had just said. As this was happening, Frank just cowered, looking down in despair.

This barrage of criticism from Mario, with support from Hilda and passive acceptance by Frank, exemplifies the family's definition of Frank as IP.

The fact that Mario spoke first, that he spoke for a long time, and that Hilda attempted to ally with Mario by supporting what he said verified the therapist's initial assumption that Mario had the "power" role in the family. Although the mother-son dyad frequently conspired to make him ineffective, the mother also sought the father's support and therefore often allied with him.

Mario then attacked Hilda for her inability to control Frank. In her own defense Hilda said that Mario had not given her enough support and had gotten involved too late.

Mario was making Hilda a seconday IP, thus reflecting flexibility in the family system. While Hilda's defense has merit, why did she not try to involve him earlier?

At this point Elsa, the daughter, became involved. She said, "Mother, you should have told Father from the beginning" and "Father, you have to give Frank a chance; he is, after all, going to college and trying to keep a job, and you don't see him involved in stealing or gangs." Mario repeated that Frank's drug use was causing problems. Hilda said nothing.

Elsa confronted the power structure and supported the IP without being attacked herself. She managed to accomplish this challenge by expressing herself in a caring, concerned way. The therapist noted several things about this interaction. First, it showed that there was love in the family and that everyone responded to it. Second, it reflected a certain amount of family flexibility. Both the love and the flexibility were very favorable prognostic signs. Finally, the therapist noted that Elsa might be a useful therapeutic ally.

At this point the therapist returned the conversation to Mario. First, the therapist shared with him some of their mutual experiences in the Cuban revolution, particularly enhancing the qualities of commitment, astuteness, and persistence needed to have gotten through that most difficult experience.

The therapist began to join Mario by emphasizing their similarities. The therapist purposefully avoided joining around qualities of machismo or militarism because it was these very qualities that separated the father from the rest of the family. The joining here was also a reframing, since the father was relabeled as a person capable of being instrumental, smart, and able to cope, rather than as a tyrannical dictator. Note that even though this was the therapist's first interaction with Mario and that his primary goal was to join Mario, the therapist had already begun some restructuring (i.e., the reframing). In order to join the father, another therapist might have used any of a number of experiences the therapist and father shared, such as being a father, having teenagers in the house, or whatever else they had in common. It is essential at this stage and throughout therapy that the therapist stay alert for and make use of whatever opportunities develop.

The therapist also talked with Mario about his feelings regarding his family's problems. The therapist empathized with the father around the pain and disappointment he was experiencing.

This was another joining tactic that also included reframing. In a subtle way it also made Mario a symptom bearer (IP). This reframing helped to hook Mario into the therapeutic process and away from the blaming process by pointing out how he was suffering and could look forward to therapy as being of value to him personally.

Another option that the therapist had at this time would have been to immediately join Elsa. Her positive functioning was so apparent and she was offering so many therapeutic options that there was a temptation to immediately join Elsa as a therapy ally. Instead the therapist was careful to enter the family through the existing power hierarchy which was headed by the father. Another therapist might have thought, "Elsa makes a good therapy ally; she challenges the family. I'm going to join right in with her challenges." But from a structural family therapy perspective that would have been a mistake. In our strategic approach a key point is to join the family through the existing power structure. In order to be accepted by the family, the therapist must first join in a way that supports the existing situation. Thus the therapist first joined the family through the father despite the obvious alternative of going through the daughter.

The therapist decided that OPFT rather than family therapy with the entire family would be initially preferable, because Frank's need to separate from the family was being blocked by the family. The therapist felt that OPFT would be useful for helping to draw clear boundaries between Frank and the family. In cases in which a family member needs to separate from the family, seeing the client alone can be very effective.

It becomes clear in the Alfaro Family case study that OPFT techniques are a set of tools that can be used flexibly within the BSFT framework. In Silvia's case it was clearly necessary to use OPFT because the family was not available for participation in treatment. On the other hand, in Frank's case a decision was made to use OPFT techniques primarily because separating Frank from the family was a therapeutic goal that would be facilitated by the use of OPFT techniques. In Frank's case the use of conjoint and one person approaches in intervention is not unlike the way most therapists use various strategies from their bag of tools.

The therapist moved over to sit by Frank. "Frank, see if you agree with me. You and I will work on some of these issues we've been discussing, but since your whole family needs to help us in getting these things taken care of, you will be in charge of taking back home what we do in therapy for the rest of them." Frank agreed. Mario disagreed, saying that he would like to be more involved. The therapist said that he would like to try this since Mario himself so rightly had said that Frank was getting older and needed to become more responsible. The therapist also reassured the family that they could all meet together again whenever it seemed appropriate.

By changing his seat to be next to Frank, the therapist joined him and gave him some power. Note how the brief joining the therapist did with Frank during their telephone conversation allowed the therapist to move quickly at this point. The therapist simultaneously emphasized Frank's adulthood and tracked Mario toward accepting the type of therapy situation that the therapist felt was appropriate. In this way Frank was designated as the OP. This placed boundaries around him and helped to encourage his independence.

Session 2 (One Person Session)

From the previous session it was clear that Frank was in the double bind of being both in conflict with and dependent upon his father. The therapist chose to work first on disengaging Frank from this double bind. It is characteristic of both BSFT and OPFT to have a specific plan for each therapy session, although there has to be flexibility to deal with any issues as they come up.

The therapist began by drawing for Frank a map of the family on the blackboard (see Fig. 9.1) and pointed out to him what a disadvantaged position he had.

This didactic technique is used frequently as an intrapersonal restructuring strategy in OPFT cases. It helps in clarifying and focusing the work that needs to be done. The therapist was helped by the information gathered from the family task to accurately depict the family interaction in a Family Map.

While sharing this perspective, the therapist said, "I didn't want to say this in front of the family, but I can't understand why you let yourself be the family's punching bag." Frank retorted, "What the heck can I do about it?"

While this is a confrontive technique, the therapist felt comfortable using it. He had already joined Frank on two previous occasions, and even though challenging, it solidified the therapist's alliance with Frank by expressing empathy for Frank's position in the family. This technique also escalated Frank's awareness of his own discomfort to the point that he was ready to consider changing his situation.

The therapist suggested that Frank change his job. This would mean that his father would not have to suprevise Frank so closely nor would

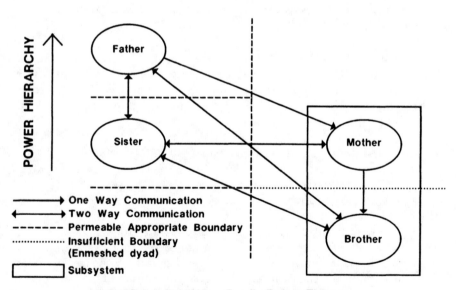

FIGURE 9.1 The Alfaro Family Before Therapy

his father need to fear that Frank's behavior would reflect on his own position at work. Frank immediately expressed concern about finding another job and questioned how his father would react to the change.

The therapist was not afraid to make a very direct suggestion rather than spend a great deal of time and effort having Frank come up with a solution of his own. To further the effort to separate Frank from his family, the therapist explored a task that would involve Frank's obtaining a job away from his father.

The therapist agreed with both of these concerns and suggested they tackle the second one first. They tried different role plays regarding how Frank might tell his father that he was going to change jobs. Using role play, the therapist told Frank to imagine a conversation with his father and then to alternate playing both himself and his father. As himself, Frank began by hemming and hawing; he sounded tentative, scared, childish. In response, as his father, he burst out with, "You can't even blow your own nose" and went on with critical remarks about why Frank could not change jobs. The therapist addressed Frank as his father and asked him what was making him respond this way: "Look at your son as he is talking to you; what's going on there, what do you see?"

Intrapersonal restructuring is a frequently used strategy for interpersonal restructuring.

After a short while Frank (as his father) said, "He can't even talk to me like a man. He mumbles, doesn't know what he wants to say." The therapist said, "That's it, Frank; you can't ask to be treated as an adult when you're acting like a kid." They then proceeded to practice how an adult would make this proposition.

Frank achieved some awareness of how he was contributing to his father's making him the IP.
Frank was then ready for practicing an interpersonal change: How would he confront his father?

To deal with Frank's first concern and to refrain from challenging his father's power too much, the therapist suggested that Frank offer his father an advisory position in getting and holding another job. The therapist and Frank therefore practiced having Frank tell his father that he would need his help in finding and doing well on another job. By doing this, Frank's leaving his job with his father would not be as great a challenge to his father's power, nor would it mean a loss of face in the family. The payoff benefit to be gained by Mario in letting go of his son a little was that he would no longer need to worry about his own job's being jeopardized by Frank.

Frank now felt comfortable with the idea of changing jobs, and his homework task was to talk with his father at home.

> *The therapist made another direct suggestion, to expedite matters.*
>
> *It is important that, as much as possible, each family member feel that changes in interactions will benefit him or her personally. Thus the therapist was careful to coach Frank through role play to frame his planned interaction with his father in a way that kept the father in a powerful position, hence tracking the power hierarchy of the family.*
>
> *It should be noted that his intervention had a dual impact— it removed Frank from a psychologically damaging work situation, and the way it was accomplished moved Frank to a more adult role in the family. It also should be noted that even though Frank was 19, he still needed some support and guidance from his family. The fact that Mario's advisory role was not a mere gesture probably contributed to Mario's accepting it without resentment.*

Session 3 (One Person Session)

Frank reported that he was successful in getting his father to help him, although they were still busy looking for another job for Frank. The therapist then asked Frank if there was anything specific he would like to work on. Since Frank had nothing, the therapist said that he would like to continue with the general issue they had dealt with last time, namely Frank's immature behavior. "Even though you're 19, there are times you act like a 12- or 13-year-old," the therapist said; "for example, there's the mess you leave your room in and the way you're handling things at school."

> *The therapist must, of course, check on the success of the previous session's homework assignment as a way of continuously reassessing the initial diagnosis of the family as well as to work on any difficulties that were encountered. Since in this case the homework had been carried out successfully, the therapist continued with his plan.*

Frank replied, "Oh, mother bitches a lot, but she takes care of my room." The therapist pointed out that this also meant she could easily pry into Frank's privacy. "Like the time she'd discovered the items you'd rather not share with her. So either you can be grown up and take care of your own room, or you can be a kid and have no privacy." Frank had a decision to make, and they worked on his ambivalence about it.

> *Note that although his mother complained, she continued to ensure that Frank's room was neat and clean and thereby helped to perpetuate his childish messiness.*
> *The therapist needed to alter this interactional pattern. He began by emphasizing how the interaction had a negative effect on Frank's life, that is, by changing Frank's perspective of the interaction—an intrapersonal change through reframing.*

The therapist had Frank stand in two different corners of the room. In one corner he was asked to experience and report everything he had felt in his current situation of no privacy, with his mother taking care of his room. In the other corner he experienced what it would be like to have increased privacy by taking care of his room himself. As it happened, Frank was very active romantically and sexually and was greatly embarrassed when his mother had found a love letter and had yelled at him when she found a package of condoms in his bureau. He decided therefore that he would prefer the privacy and should begin taking care of his room himself.

> *This is a variation on role play borrowed from Gestalt therapy that was used to achieve the necessary intrapersonal change in Frank.*

The homework task was for him to begin to take care of his room, although the therapist warned Frank that his mother would probably try to prevent it and that he must not permit this to happen.

> *This was a relatively easy change for Frank to make. The possibility of his mother sabotaging it existed but did not seem strong enough for the therapist to spend time rehearsing ways to overcome it.*

Session 4 (One Person Session)

Frank came in happily announcing that he had gotten a job in the same line of business though working for another company. Besides helping

Frank make the contacts that led to his new job, Frank said that his father was giving him hints on how to deal in his very tough and competitive new position. The therapist pointed out to Frank that he had been successful in changing the affective tone of his relationship with his father. Frank agreed but complained that his father was still on his back about college grades. The therapist pointed out to Frank that he was doing poorly in college and said that he could not understand how such a smart person got such poor grades.

> *Frank was so proud and happy about his new job that the therapist chose to track this rather than ask Frank about the homework task of cleaning his room.*
>
> *The father had maintained his position of power but was now using that role to help Frank develop his independence.*
>
> *The therapist also attempted to reframe Frank's perception of himself as a "smart person."*

A review of the situation suggested that his drug use was interfering with his studies. Frank responded that he had to party sometime. The therapist asked Frank with whom he partied. Frank replied that he partied with his friends, but lately, most frequently with his steady girl, Vicky. The therapist encouraged Frank to tell him more about this Vicky. Frank shared how much he liked her, how they got along so well and enjoyed each other's company, and how sexually excited he was with her and that they had a good time making love. The therapist commented, "It sounds to me like you might be getting serious in this part of your life also." Frank smiled and chuckled and quickly replied, "No, don't worry, I'm not ready for marriage yet," to which the therapist quickly responded, "Well, maybe not marriage but at least it sounds like you're ready to start enjoying a woman more fully than simple adolescent games." Frank agreed that his relationship with Vicky was very special and he felt good about it.

> *The therapist further strengthened Frank by reframing Frank's perception of himself from "partying" to being "serious" about life.*

The therapist then wondered, "Speaking of relationships, what part does your relationship to marijuana play in this love affair of yours? I mean, I *know* what part it has played in the past in your relationship with your parents, but I'm curious about you, Vicky, and 'Mary Jane.'" Now the therapist really had Frank's attention, "What do you mean, you know what part it played in my relationship with my parents? It doesn't have anything to do with them. I just like it, period." Authoritatively, the therapist went on, "No, I know too much about kids, drugs, parents, and so forth to buy that simple answer. I also know you and your family too well now to miss the obvious. Let's face it, Frank, you and practically every other kid in the world need to establish your own identities, rebel, do your own thing, but in your case even more so because your Dad's been so domineering. So I know that although marijuana may feel good sometimes, it's also been your way of rebelling and letting your parents get it where it really hurts. After all, you know as well as I do that practically nothing can bother conservative Cuban parents more than their kid's being involved in drugs. In that sense I can understand why you use it. I just wonder what part it plays now that you are in some real ways becoming more adult and independent."

> *The therapist had tracked Frank from his success in finding a new job through another topic of concern to his father, his school grades, and from there to Frank's relationship with Vicky. The therapist framed Frank's feelings about Vicky as another measure of his "growing up" and, in this light, confronted him with the role of drugs. This confrontation was done from a position of alliance with Frank and concern about how drugs may be working "against him" instead of "for him." The therapist also took the opportunity to reframe Frank's use of drugs as a sign of adolescent rebelliousness and wondered how at this point, when he was becoming an adult, drugs might "boomerang" against him. That is, Frank may have used drugs as a way of acting out his conflict with his parents. The therapist, however, strategically shifted the focus by asserting that drugs may also be triangulated in Frank's relationship to Vicky. In this way Frank may be made more willing to explore the negative consequences drug use has for him.*

Again Frank stuck to his story: "Well, I just do it when we go out, and I really enjoy myself." The therapist wondered, "Have you ever tried enjoying yourself with Vicky without the dope?" Frank answered, "No, I don't see the point of it since I like it that way." "Well," the therapist said, "you're really not in a position to judge unless you compare. I tell you, if you think sex is good while doped, you should try it without; then you'll really know what fully enjoying a woman is all about. As a matter of fact, if you're so sure, I'll make you a bet: I'll give you a really special homework assignment for this week. I want you to try sex with grass once and then try sex without grass a couple of days later. You'll see how much more fully aware of every sense, every experience, and every feeling you are without it. If you don't come back agreeing with me, then we may need to worry about your own natural sex drive and sexuality." Frank laughed (nervously) and, of course, agreed to this task. As he was about to leave the therapist joked, "Isn't life funny? First, grass is like your ally in rebelling against your parents, then it turns into your competitor in relating to Vicky. Well, I don't know about you, but when it comes to love and sex, I sure don't like triangles. I like my woman to be the only other one in the picture." Frank wanted to continue to talk about this, however, the therapist purposely cut him off, saying, "Look, Frank, I refuse to get into the same role as your father, where I say don't do it and you're going to do it. I insist on treating you as an adult. You've got the facts. You make the decision."

The therapist presented Frank with a paradox through a task that, because it was paradoxical, could not fail. If Frank failed to carry it out, he would be tacitly admitting that the therapist may be right after all. If Frank carried it out and reported that sex with drugs is better, he would be admitting that something was sexually wrong with him and thus that he needed drugs to help him sexually. If Frank carried it out and liked sex without drugs better, then, of course, the need or desire for grass would be questioned and probably reduced or eliminated. The therapist set the task in a manner wherein the expectation was that sex without dope is much more pleasurable and adult.

"As a matter of fact," the therapist continued, "if you really mean that using drugs has nothing to do with you and your parents, then make sure that when you do drugs your parents have absolutely no way of knowing that you've used them. What I mean is, be the only grown-up in charge of supervising your drug use."

This intervention furthered the process of Frank's being responsible for himself and forced him to confront his drug use as an issue independent of his relationship with his parents.

This strategic therapeutic maneuver, targeted directly at the drug use, accomplished three related objectives. First, it was targeted at disengaging Frank from parental authority on the issue of drug taking, thus eliminating the possibility of this act's being rebellious or aggressive to his parents. Second, it manipulated Frank into a position where he was answerable only to himself. Third, the therapist attempted to eliminate some of the secondary gains that drug use may have provided by detriangulating drug use from family conflicts.

Session 5 (One Person Session)

The session began with Frank announcing that he had done his "most enjoyable" homework task and bragging to the therapist with macho bravado that he was quite a good lover even without the grass. "I don't need no dope to really get it on, so you don't have to worry about me having any sex problems."

The therapist praised him and wondered what Vicky's reaction was. Frank grudgingly admitted that she did say that she felt they were both more romantic about it. The therapist then questioned, "Well, which way are you going to go? Are you going to let Vicky and you decide what you enjoy best, or let grass be in charge?" Frank then began a whole speech about how he was not an addict and he could take it or leave it. The therapist then set up a Gestalt experiment in which Frank and grass had a dialogue, with Frank alternatively playing each part. The beginning sentence was guided by the therapist: "Frank, be grass first and say to Frank, 'I know you need me to really feel good.'" When Frank reluctantly first spoke those words, he quickly then shifted to the Frank position and retorted, "You're full of sh . . . [pause.] This is ridiculous. Grass is just grass. You use it when you want to." The therapist insisted he continue by being grass again, feeling how powerful and important grass felt about itself, how sure of its hold on Frank (as it looked upon him). Frank did so then, as "grass" said, "You've got to admit it, Frank, I've given you a lot of good times and made you feel good about yourself and about life."

The therapist asked Frank to switch to the role of Frank and explore his reaction to this confrontation before responding. Frank then said, "Well, this is ridiculous. I can have good sex without you. I can have friends and fun without you. You're at my service, not the other way around." The therapist quickly intervened: "I'll believe it when I see it. Except for our little sex experiment, it seems to me grass has been the boss and you the servant. As a matter of fact, it has the power to make you not care about being labeled a screw-up, a no-good. It even interferes with your career goals." The therapist added, "About the only good thing here is that since you were originally in charge of calling the shots, you can always put yourself in charge again by 'putting grass in its place.'" Frank thought, then challenged, "I'll show you who's in charge. I'll only use it every once in a while on weekends when I'm out with the guys." The therapist congratulated him and added, "Well, I guess it's progress if you decide to be grown up during the week and with Vicky, and a dependent child only on weekends with the guys."

The therapist set up a Gestalt experiment similar to the one Frank had experienced earlier in exploring his relationship to his father. Here, the therapist wanted Frank to similarly experience the position of powerlessness he held vis-à-vis grass—in other words, how he had transferred the dependency on his father to a dependency on grass, rendering him unable or incapable of calling his own shots. Progressively the therapist worked on increasing Frank's ability to assume control over his own life.

The reader should note that addictive behaviors may reflect maladaptive interpersonal patterns as well as intrapersonal conflicts. In the case of Frank, both were true. Frank may have used drugs, at least partially, as a way of making a statement of rebellion against the unreasonable developmental level he held in the family. Once the interpersonal aspect had been addressed, however, the therapist also had to work on the intrapersonal struggle between the object of addiction and the addict. In the intrapersonal sense, drug use is a behavior that occurs compulsively when the addict has surrendered certain aspects of his life to the object of addiction. The myth of the addict is that the object can do for him what he alone cannot do for himself. The purpose of the intrapersonal portion of the therapy, then, is to provide for the addict experiences that help regain power over his or her life. The experience that will allow him to regain power is one that first gets the addict in touch with his or her powerlessness. Recognizing this powerlessness, the addict feels threatened by it and reacts against it. Reacting against the powerlessness represents regaining control over the addictive behavior and thus over the self.

The therapist did not want to go back on the position he had taken in the previous session of not lecturing Frank. The little joke framed Frank's behavior in just the right way, while allowing the decision and choice to rest on Frank's shoulders.

The therapist then asked about the homework task from two weeks ago, Frank's cleaning his own room. Frank reported that that was not going so well. When he started to do it, his mother told him not to bother since he was so tired and she could take care of it. The therapist reminded Frank that in the first session his mother had expressed her frustration at being "only" a housewife and had said that she wanted to get out and do something different.

Frank's mother sabotaged a change that she had said she wanted. In structural terms this would be seen as the system's homeostasis resisting any change and as his mother fearing the loss of her primary family role—protective mother. One of the difficulties in working primarily with one person is that the therapist does not have direct access to other family members and hence cannot intervene directly to prevent sabotage to desired behavior change in the IP/OP.

At this point the therapist introduced to Frank the idea that it was in his own best interest that his mother should be relieved of household chores and given an opportunity to pursue career interests.

Going to the blackboard, the therapist drew a map of the family's interactions (Fig. 9.2) in which it was evident that his mother was overly involved with Frank as a substitute for her own personal pursuits and as a detour to avoid conflict with his father regarding the issue of her working. His father, in turn, used Frank and his troubles as a means of postponing this confrontation with his wife. The result was that Frank was triangulated because he was being used by both parents to avoid confronting their problems with each other. Such triangulation made it impossible for Frank to distance himself sufficiently to effect a successful individuation.

The therapist planned to work (through Frank) on giving Hilda a new, more constructive role. But first, as usual, some intrapersonal change in Frank had to be accomplished.

The therapist used the didactic technique of mapping the family again. The mapping becomes a strategy for facilitating the process of "splitting the executive observant ego." In this fashion Frank was able to gain perspective and observe the family's interactions, including his participation in them.

The therapist joined Frank as a salesman and said, "Now it is my turn to sell, and I want to sell you the idea that it would be profitable for you to set things up in such a way that your father and mother are dealing more with each other about this and other things and that they deal less with you." Frank liked this idea and welcomed the thought of his own freedom but questioned how he could ever accomplish it.

The therapist tracked a language familiar to Frank, that of sales.

The therapist went back to the board and pointed to the position of the sister, Elsa, saying, "Here's your helper!" The therapist explained that an alliance with Elsa would be beneficial in two respects: (1) It would identify Frank with someone in the family who was respected and problem free, and (2) it would give him the necessary assistant

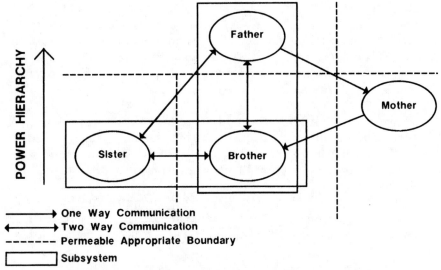

POWER HIERARCHY

——————➤ One Way Communication
◄——————➤ Two Way Communication
-------- Permeable Appropriate Boundary
☐ Subsystem

FIGURE 9.2 The Alfaro family after four therapy sessions.

labor to free his mother from household chores. Frank saw the value of this alliance with Elsa, and he and the therapist role played ways in which he could get his sister "sold" on this, appealing to the sister's genuine concern for both mother and Frank. Thus Frank's task was rehearsed, and he was ready to carry it out. When he had been successful in recruiting Elsa, they would devise a list of chores that they could do between them.

> *Here the therapist make use of Elsa as a therapeutic ally. Note that in other circumstances (i.e., if the sister were less insightful, capable, caring, or willing to work), a great deal more preparatory work might have been necessary to achieve this amount of cooperation with another family member.*

Session 6 (Conjoint Session)

A couple of days after session 5, Frank called the therapist and told him that although things were going well on his homework tasks, the family was in an uproar because he had been fired from his new job. Even though he had been fired due to company cutbacks, the family, or at least his mother, saw his being fired as a failure on his part. Because of the crisis the therapist rescheduled session 6 to be a conjoint family session with the whole family present.

*Crises are to be expected during therapy. A distinguishing char-
acteristic of a skilled therapist is that she or he will see these as
opportunities and make use of them for therapeutic purposes
rather than thinking of them as setbacks. They are opportunities
since they indicate that the usual family structure has become
unbalanced and therefore easier to change. These are often excellent opportunities to have a conjoint session.*

When the family arrived, the mother began complaining that she had
at first thought things were going better, but that she no longer felt that
way. "Look what Frank's done to us now." At that point, Frank said,
"Mother, how many times do I have to explain to you that it's not my
fault?"

The father quickly allied with Frank, explaining to his wife that it
was a tough business and that the company was having a hard time.
They had to let some people go, and it had just been a matter of last
hired, first fired.

*What a change! Frank and his father were now allies. The
conjoint session gave the therapist an opportunity to identify that
important progress had been made with this family.*

The mother continued to make Frank the identified patient, saying
he was irresponsible, not telling her what he was doing and so on. A
heated argument ensued involving the mother, the father, and Frank,
wherein Frank and the mother complained about each other and the
father ended by throwing his hands up and said, "This is the kind of
thing that goes on in my home all the time! I want some peace and
quiet!"

The therapist turned to the daughter, Elsa. "It seems to me that your
mother is overwhelmed and very anxious. If you think I'm right, maybe
you can get her to talk to you about that." Elsa agreed, indicating that
she had been noticing that for a long time, and turned to the mother
with loving support: "Mother, what's the matter?" Although initially
the mother insisted on defining the problem in terms of her concern
about Frank, the therapist reminded Hilda that Frank was an adult and
should be left to take care of himself; she needed to think of her own
well-being. At this she admitted to feeling frustrated and bored, especially now that the kids were getting older and recently had even been
trying to help around the house. The therapist explained that this
moment in the family's life was a time of transition and invited the
family to suggest ways in which a new adaptation could be made. The
father said, "I know what she [Hilda] really wants. She wants to go out

and work." Frank jumped in, saying, "I don't see why she can't do that. We're old enough to take care of ourselves now." Discussion ensued, with both Frank and Elsa supporting their mother in her attempts to convince the father that she could seek employment.

The therapist challenged the way the family was framing the situation, through the therapeutic ally, Elsa.

Note that the therapist continued to require that everyone think of Frank as an adult, that they give up their old view of him as a child. Moreover, he used the opportunity given by the conjoint session to work on his goal of changing Hilda's role in the family.

Also note that Frank changed alliances from his father to his mother. This flexibility was a sign of improved family health, since only Elsa had shown such flexibility in the first session. Also, progress was evidenced by the family's confrontation of a problem that had been buried previously.

The therapist said, "If mother is working, the way you guys have been spoiled, the house will be a mess in a week." Based on his previous work with the therapist, Frank took the lead in suggesting ways of overcoming these objections, such as ways to distribute household chores. Elsa supported Frank.

In this discussion, since the father was the only family member objecting to the plan, the therapist took the position of apparently allying with the father in voicing objections. This was done as a manipulation to put pressure on the system to produce specific, realistic ways through which the major change of having mother work could be accomplished. It also prevented the father from becoming too defensive and thereby taking an intractable position that might block accomplishment of this change.

The therapist then turned to the father and said, "Perhaps you ought to reconsider, 'cause it seems to me you might have at least a couple of things to gain: extra income and more time with a happier wife."

The therapist could appear to be persuaded at this point. He tried something new by modeling a different attitude that allied the therapist with the rest of the family. Perhaps to his own surprise, Mario found himself at least temporarily persuaded.

"You guys have convinced me. How about it, Mario, do you think this is workable?" Mario agreed to "give it a try."

Another major event had occurred. Not only had an issue been confronted, it had been resolved as well.

The therapist ended the session by saying that he would continue to work with Frank to resolve his problems. Frank, in turn, would keep the therapist abreast of the family's progress.

This statement served to strengthen Frank's position in the family as an independent adult as well as a therapeutic agent. It also relieved the family of the task of parenting Frank (since the therapist would be working on "Frank's problem").

This conjoint session served several useful functions for the therapist. It verified that Frank and Mario had become allies, that flexibility had improved, and that the family was more willing to confront problems. Further, with some help from the therapist the family had been able to actually resolve a conflict and had moved toward changing Hilda's role in the family.

Session 7 (One Person Session)

Frank reported that through his father's contacts he had found another job. The therapist then asked how the family was doing with regard to their mother's going back to work. Through a friend in the business Hilda had become interested in real estate and had just enrolled in the required real estate training courses. Chores around the house were going well, although the only thing Mario was willing to do was grocery shopping, since he liked food so much.

This session, like most of the previous sessions, took place within a week and was used to consolidate gains from the conjoint session, particularly regarding Frank's individuation. Because so much progress had already taken place, from this point on the therapist began to make the time between sessions longer. The strategy of spacing the time between sessions in BSFT is part of the beginning of the termination process. The initial session sets into motion the restructuring strategies. The additional time between later sessions provides the opportunity for these changes to take place at a natural pace. Thus while termination is not as significant an issue in BSFT as it ought to be in longer therapies, it is nevertheless attended to. The longer time between later sessions marks the beginning of and helps to prepare for termination.

The therapist asked, "How does it feel to have all that pressure from the family off your back?" Frank said that it was a great relief. The therapist then said, "I don't think it is such a hot deal, because if things go wrong in your life, you have no one to blame except yourself. If you really want to take care of yourself, you should depend more on your parents like you had been doing before." Frank said that he could take care of himself, but the therapist continued to push: "I'll believe it when I see it . . . like how much drugs are you using now?"

The therapist forced Frank to defend his new patterns of interaction and to solidify the goals he had set for himself. This type of "reverse psychology" or paradoxical technique is sometimes used to promote reframing and restructuring generally.

Frank reported that he was getting serious with his girlfriend Vicky and had given up marijuana entirely because he did not want to disappoint her. In terms of school, he was still thinking about what to do since he liked working and thought that college might not be the way for him to go. The therapist said that Frank did have a lot of pressure. His job as a salesman, family responsibilities, his relationship with Vicky, plus college, altogether seemed like quite a load. The therapist wondered to what degree his use of cocaine might be one of the ways he was trying to handle so much.

The therapist was supporting and tracking Frank again.

The therapist said, "Let's try to put all these pressures around the room, and going from one to the other see how it feels to try to handle them without using cocaine." Frank went around the room, directed by the therapist, to handle and attend to each and every one of these tasks. It was not long before Frank stood in the middle, turned to the therapist, and said, "This is too damn much!" The therapist sat Frank next to him and said, "I agree with you. You notice that even snorting your way from one task to the next one doesn't solve the problem, though." Frank responded that he really wanted to give up college. "There are other ways to make it financially in this world, but Dad will have a fit."

This is another technique borrowed from Gestalt therapy that was used to achieve intrapersonal change by having the individual "visualize" and clarify his experience.

It was time to end the session. The therapist suggested that during the week Frank needed to think about whether he was going to be man enough to confront his father or continue to "run around like a maniac, dependent on coke."

As with the earlier decision regarding drug use, the therapist wanted to leave Frank with a heightened tension around this issue of giving up college. At this point the therapist felt that Frank probably should give up college, but the decision had to be Frank's alone.

Session 8 (One Person Session)

Frank had made up his mind. He wanted to drop out of college and go for a special junior executive training program at the regional electrical power company. He saw this as a longterm career opportunity. He and Vicky had become more serious about getting married, even though it was a little risky. Frank said that these were two big pieces of news to give to the family and he was going to need the therapist's help in doing it. The therapist agreed to help and asked Frank to first of all report on how the family was doing.

This session was scheduled 2 weeks after the last session, and important decisions had been made in the interim.

The therapist thought it would be useful to have Frank go to the blackboard and draw a map of his perception of how the family was organized now (Fig. 9.3), while simultaneously reporting orally. The family situation that surfaced was one wherein Frank was no longer triangulated, was in a more powerful independent position, and saw his parents as closer together (they went shopping together and had gone on a couple of "dates").

This exercise helped Frank to gain an awareness of his new, more adult, and strong position in the family. He needed this sense in order to gain confidence to tell his parents about his plans.

The therapist commented, "From what you've given me here, we're not talking about a kid rebelling against his parents' wishes but rather one adult talking to other adults about his life goals." Frank experienced this difference with satisfaction. To avoid any possibility of triangulating and to reinforce the parents' spousal boundaries, the therapist suggested to Frank that he should tell his parents together. A further

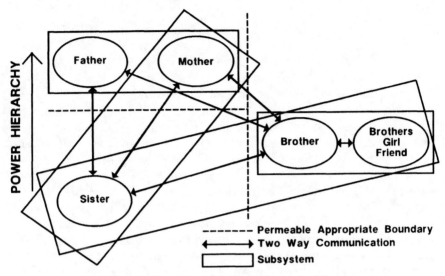

FIGURE 9.3 The Alfaro family at the end of therapy.

suggestion was made that Frank share the news with Elsa first, to strengthen the sibling alliance in case her support was needed.

The therapist continued to reframe Frank's view of himself. Note that Frank had become such a sophisticated therapeutic agent that the therapist was able to discuss relatively abstract concepts with him.

Although the therapist gave Frank some direction, he no longer felt that extensive practice of the interaction Frank was to have with his parents would be necessary. Once again, this example of the therapist moving out while placing greater responsibility in Frank further illustrates the ongoing process of termination at this stage of the therapy.

Note that termination as practiced in BSFT is distinguished from termination in nonstructural, verbal therapies. While a verbal therapist might discuss termination, structural therapists, in addition to verbal discussions about therapy, also build termination structurally into the therapy. Thus, for example, termination is reflected first in the lengthening of the time between sessions and subsequently in a shifting of therapeutic responsibility from the therapist back to the OP or the family.

Session 9 (One Person Session)

Frank reported that he told his parents together about his decisions. Elsa was supportive, and his parents accepted his decisions. He continued to report on other areas in which he was making progress. To be admitted to the junior executive program, he had to pass some tests. His score was sufficiently high that he was one of only 5 selected from a group of over 100 candidates. Upon questioning, he proudly announced he had not used any cocaine when taking the test, and as a matter of fact, he had not used any for some time. The therapist asked if he had noticed any improvement in his sex life since he quit drugs. Frank just grinned. More seriously, he added that he and Vicky were discussing a date for their marriage. The therapist continued to keep this session light and commented to Frank about how much growth he had achieved and how much more adult he had become. The therapist wondered how this might be affecting the family. Frank said that his mother was now responding well, since she was very enthusiastic about her real estate sales training. His father, however, seemed to be edgy and complained that everyone in the family was always running off to one thing or another. The therapist then said that it sounded as if things were progressing well.

> *This session occurred 1 month after the last session.*
> *The therapist was tracking and supporting Frank's success.*

The therapist added that it would be good for him to meet with the whole family to discuss Frank's plans for the future. The therapist therefore asked Frank to notify the family members that they should all come, as the therapist needed to review their views and opinions regarding Frank's goals.

> *At this point an individually oriented therapist might help Frank to disown responsibility for his parents' readjustment and instead to focus on his own needs and goals with greater commitment. However, if a therapist thinks in a family systems way, she or he must bear in mind that systems can be very powerful and effective in creating a crisis in order to, in this case, prevent Frank from making the final break. That is, unless the system has been helped to restructure effectively to ensure that everyone's needs are met, the changes made will not be permanent. Frank was very central before, and he could easily be repositioned as an IP again to effect an immobilization that would keep the family's homeostasis.*

In light of this, the therapist decided that the whole family should be seen conjointly the following week. It was important that although at this point the therapist saw that the marital couple (parents) needed to be the focus of therapy at the next session, the message be carried to them by Frank in a manner that still signaled that Frank was the apparent focus of therapeutic concern. This avoided any possibility of resistance on the part of the parents.

Session 10 (Conjoint Session)

The therapist began by questioning the family members on their views and opinions of Frank's plans and decisions. The father immediately responded by saying that Frank's improvement was good and he hoped it would continue, but he wondered if Frank was really ready to take on this junior executive position and was really responsible enough for marriage. "After all," Mario said, "not too long ago he couldn't even keep up his room and get to work on time."

Manipulatively, the therapist asked the mother, "Well, for your sake I hope Frank is ready, 'cause I imagine you are eager now to have more time for your own career." As expected, Hilda agreed with the therapist and added, "Sometimes I think Mario wants Frank to stay a kid forever just to keep me home." The therapist wondered about this, but Mario denied "such nonsense."

The therapist jokingly asked Elsa, "As the expert family observer, what do you think? Is it true your Dad prefers for your mother to stay home?" Elsa tellingly refused to get involved and stated, "That's one fight I'm not going to get into, but I sure hope they'll straighten it out soon."

The therapist's plan was to begin the session with his "excuse" for bringing the family into the therapy session. He would then move as quickly as possible to the husband–wife relation. The therapist purposefully moved Mario's question over to Hilda, hoping she would disagree and thus establish a conflictual stance between the parents.

The therapist made a serious error by trying to triangulate Elsa with her parents. Fortunately Elsa did not get caught up in it.

The therapist agreed and asked Elsa and Frank to wait outside while he worked with the parents alone.

The interactions that followed clarified to the therapist Mario's concern about emotional distance from his wife and their inability to substitute new interactions as their parenting functions diminished. To relieve their anxiety, the therapist explained to them that it is very common for couples to become so involved with parenting that when their children grow up, they have to work at reestablishing themselves as husband and wife. He said that Frank had told him that they had been on a few "dates" and that this was just the right sort of thing they needed to do in order to get to know each other as spouses again.

To clearly draw boundaries between the children and parents on this issue and to ensure more intense and concentrated work by the spouses, the therapist decided to separate them from the younger people. Since the therapist was following a strategic, problem-focused approach, and since "Frank's problems" had been largely resolved, he could now lend some support and guidance to the spousal subsystem. However, given the time limitations, in-depth marital therapy was not possible.

The therapist then asked them to make plans to spend more time together. They agreed on a date. However this did not seem to be sufficient. Mario commented that they did not seem to have anything in common anymore; unless they talked about the kids, they did not really have anything to say to each other. The therapist suggested that perhaps he should let his wife tell him about her real estate plans. He may not know anything about real estate, but "business is business and real estate is big business." He had been out in the business world for a long time, while she had been at home. Therefore she was going to need his help in just the same way Frank had. Mario seemed pleased with this idea.

Following typical structural family therapy practice, the therapist had Mario and Hilda conduct an actual interaction in front of him (making a date in this case). In this instance the therapist could observe that "dating" was not sufficient for Mario and Hilda.

At this point the therapist reframed by stating that he thought that Mario's concern was not that the children at home would not be properly taken care of (as he had been indicating earlier) but rather that he and his wife might drift apart. The therapist agreed that this was a valid and important concern and encouraged them to discuss together ways in which this could be avoided.

At the end of this session the therapist said that he wanted to see just the two of them together, "since Frank is doing so well."

The therapist had realized Mario's "real" concern much earlier but had not wanted to confront him. Confronting him might have led to his becoming so defensive that further work would have been difficult. The therapist had prepared him by already suggesting a solution. Further, the therapist tracked Mario into accepting his "real" concern through the therapist's reframing rather than through a stressful confrontation.

This last statement was made to signal the end of the IPhood of Frank.

Sessions with family subsystems (the spousal subsystem in this case) can be very useful in some cases.

Session 11 (Spousal Subsystem)

The 11th session was to be focused around ways in which the couple could begin to restructure their lives, now that Frank was on his way out of the home and Elsa was becoming more independent all the time.

The therapist began by asking what Mario and Hilda had discussed alone together. He called this a "reacquaintance." Smilingly, Mario corrected the therapist, stating, "Really, it's not a reacquaintance. In some ways it's more like getting to know a person for the first time. I never knew Hilda had a business woman in her."

The therapist encouraged the couple to see each other again as sort of "newlyweds," in that their task was to make new adjustments to each other and to their "new" family life. There was some light humor about dating and "sex after 40." In the end, Mario suggested that the best way he could think of helping Hilda in that "rough business world out there" was for him also to get a real estate license and for them to go into business together.

This was an exciting suggestion, and the therapist supported it wholeheartedly, especially since, given the nature of real estate, Mario did not have to give up his present job but could slowly move into his (their) new career(s).

In addition, since Mario did not have any special expertise or experience, he would not immediately overpower his wife in this relationship.

Session 12 (One Person)

Frank came by himself to finish the therapy sessions. He and Vicky were discussing marriage seriously and had set a tentative date of within six months. Frank told the therapist he expected him to come to the wedding. His sister was going to be a bridesmaid and his mother (as is typically the Cuban tradition) was all excited, planning wedding details. Frank had a good sense of the strength and skill he exhibited in not only being able to improve his own life but that of his whole family as well. This self-knowledge, the therapist felt, would stay with him forever.

The work of OPFT with Frank had really ended more than a month earlier. However, this session provided the therapist with an opportunity to check that Frank had maintained his progress and gave Frank closure to his therapy.

FOLLOW-UP

At the time of the 1-year follow-up, Frank and Vicky had been married and had moved into an apartment of their own. Frank was drug free and getting ahead in his career. In fact, he was making more money than the therapist, and they joked that the therapist should change jobs.

Hilda was working full time in real estate sales, with Mario helping part time. He planned to quit his other job at the end of the year in order to go into real estate full time. Elsa continued to be as healthy as ever and had become good friends with Vicky. Thus the structural changes created during therapy had been maintained and had led to improved functioning for the entire family.

Part VI

Research

10

Research on Brief Strategic Family Therapy: Treatment, Engagement, and Diagnosis

This chapter presents a brief overview of research relevant to the three major topics covered in this book: treatment, engagement, and diagnosis. Highlighted in this chapter are research studies establishing the effectiveness of the treatment approaches presented in this book, the effectiveness of structural systems engagement, and the psychometric properties of the formal method of assessment and diagnosis, the Family Tasks (FT)/SFSR. This research was conducted as part of a systematic program of studies carried out over the past decade.

TREATMENT

Two major studies funded by the National Institute of Mental Health (Grant No. 1-R01-MH34821) and the National Institute on Drug Abuse (Grant No. R18 DA03224) were conducted to test the effectiveness of BSFT and of the OPFT modality. One of these studies (Szapocznik, Rio, et al., 1987), funded by the first of these institutes, consisted of an experimental investigation with random assignment of families to one of three conditions: BSFT, individual psychodynamic child therapy, and a recreational activities control condition. Sixty-nine two-parent Hispanic families with boys ages 6 to 12 referred due to behavioral or emotional problems participated in this study. Families and IPs were extensively tested at intake, termination, and at a 1-year follow-up after the completion of treatment. Assessments included parent reports of child behaviors, children's self-reports of anxiety and depression, psychodynamic assessment of child functioning by an independent clinical psychologist, and the SFSR as a measure of family functioning.

The results of this study revealed that both treatment conditions, BSFT and individual psychodynamic child therapy, were more effective than the control condition in retaining subjects in treatment. Both treatment conditions were highly effective in bringing about lasting changes in parent reports of child behaviors, children's self-reports of anxiety and depression, and psychodynamic child functioning. In the measure of family functioning, the SFSR, there were no improvements at the time of termination. However by the time of the 1-year follow-up, the BSFT condition showed a dramatic improvement, whereas the individual psychodynamic child therapy condition showed a dramatic deterioration in family functioning. This finding is theoretically understandable from a structural systems perspective.

As we have argued all along, what sets us apart as family therapists is that we wish to maintain the interdependency of the family members whenever possible. One of the central tenets of structural family systems theory is that the IP is serving an active role in holding the family together by helping the family avoid other problems. As family therapists our response to trouble is to look to the family for help. Our aim is, first, to identify those aspects of the family's patterns of interactions that are not letting the family (and its individual members) achieve its goals, and, second, to create the opportunity for families to change these interactions, thereby preserving interdependency while exchanging unsuccessful interactions for more successful ones. Thus for this study the boys in individual psychodynamic child therapy did improve behaviorally, symptomatically, and dynamically, but their families deteriorated at follow-up, whereas in BSFT the boys improved *and* family integrity was protected. This study thus documented that BSFT not only ameliorates symptoms, but also preserves the family integrity.

The second major set of studies (Szapocznik et al., 1983; 1986), funded by the National Institute on Drug Abuse, investigated not only the effectiveness of BSFT and OPFT when used with adolescent IPs, but also some underlying theoretical assumptions of family theory and practice, that is, that the whole family must be present in order to bring about structural family change. Seventy-six Hispanic families were randomly assigned to one of two conditions: BSFT in the conjoint mode, as described in Chapter 5, or OPFT, as described in Chapter 8. Client families were extensively tested at intake, termination, and at a 6-month follow-up. The assessment battery included parental ratings of adolescent behavioral problems, independent assessments of the adolescent IP's psychosocial and psychiatric functioning, and family members' reports of family climate and family functioning as measured by the SFSR.

The results of this study revealed that both OPFT and BSFT in the conjoint mode were highly effective in bringing about and maintaining through to follow-up improvement in IP functioning, family climate, and family structural functioning. Of great significance for our work, OPFT was as effective as BSFT in the conjoint mode in bringing about and maintaining improvement in all of these outcome variables, demonstrating that it is possible to bring about change in family functioning while working primarily with one person. Hence this research clarifies that what is critical in family work is not who is present in the therapy sessions but rather how the therapist conceptualizes the problem and the intervention.

ENGAGEMENT

The effectiveness of structural systems engagement was tested in a major study funded by the National Institute of Drug Abuse (Grant No. R18 DA03224). For this study families were randomly assigned to one of two conditions: structural systems engagement and an engagement-as-usual control condition. The structural systems engagement condition was conducted as defined in Chapters 6 and 7 in this book and the engagement-as-usual condition was designed to parallel the kind of procedures typically used by drug abuse outpatient programs in encouraging clients to enter treatment. Subjects were 120 Hispanic families with an adolescent IP who was either known to be using drugs or displaying a set of predetermined high risk behaviors typically associated with drug abuse. Outcome was assessed in terms of each condition's effectiveness in bringing families into treatment and in maintaining families in treatment through completion.

The results of the study revealed that structural systems engagement was dramatically more effective than the engagement control condition. In fact, 77% of cases in the structural systems engagement condition completed treatment, versus 25% of cases in the control condition. (Note that the 25% engagement and completion rate is within the usual range for treatment programs of this kind.) Thus when resistance to entering treatment is conceptualized in structural terms, it is possible to "treat" the resistance as a symptom of the family's pattern of interactions in the same way that any other symptom is treated within a structural framework.

ASSESSMENT AND DIAGNOSIS

The psychometric properties of the SFSR were established during a series of studies conducted as part of the larger program of treatment outcome studies (Szapocznik et al., under editorial review). The studies were designed to develop and refine the normative anchors for the SFSR scales as well as to establish the factor structure, reliability, and validity of the ratings.

Factor Structure

To identify the factor structure of the SFSR, a principal components analysis of the SFSR was conducted on a sample of 311 families, yielding a two-factor solution. The first factor, which accounted for the largest percentage of the variance, was termed a relations factor because it consisted primarily of items representing family interaction. For adolescent samples this factor included structure, resonance, and flexibility. For child samples it also included developmental stage. The second factor was termed a problem factor because it consisted of items tapping how conflicts and problems are managed by the family (conflict resolution and IPhood).

Reliability

Internal consistency and interrater reliabilities were obtained. The Cronbach score alpha was used to estimate the internal consistency reliability of the SFSR. The analysis yielded a coefficient alpha of 0.97, indicating excellent internal consistency.

For the interrater reliability, two structural family therapists were trained on the use of the SFSR. Ten cases were rated independently by the two raters. Three kinds of interrater reliability were obtained: percent agreement, Pearson r, and intraclass r. For percent agreement, the two raters either completely agreed or were within one scale point of each other for all item-scales in 90% of the comparisons. The

Pearson's correlation between the raters yielded a coefficient of 0.94 for total score, 0.93 for the relations factor, and 0.85 for the problem factor. The Pearson's r for the six item-scales had a mean of 0.74. Intraclass correlation was also computed as a form of interrater reliability, yielding 0.94 for total score, 0.93 for the relations factor, and 0.87 for the problem factor. The intraclass correlation for the six item-scales had a mean of 0.67. Thus the SFSR total and factor scales have excellent interrater reliability, while the item-scales have remarkably good interrater reliabilities for single items.

Validity

In our programmatic treatment outcome studies, we have examined both the content and construct validity of the SFSR.

Content validity was built into the SFSR by developing the scales to tap structural concepts. In the course of our treatment outcome studies, a large number of research clinicians experienced in structural family therapy have contributed to the development and refinement of the content of the SFSR scales. Thus each of the dimensions of the SFSR draws upon extensive clinical experience in the systematic application of concepts central to structural family systems thinking. By utilizing this pool of clinical experience, we have sought to maximize the content validity of the SFSR.

Construct validity has been extensively examined because of the critical importance of determining whether the SFSR behaves as would be predicted by structural theory. The two treatment studies reviewed earlier in this chapter provide evidence for the sensitivity of the SFSR to change due to treatment. These studies establish both that the SFSR measures improvements that result from structural family therapy and that it discriminates between interventions that are and are not expected to bring about structural family change.

Construct validity has also been explored in a study of a structural modality known as Family Effectiveness Training (FET) (Szapocznik, Rio, Perez-Vidal, Kurtines, & Santisteban, 1984), which randomly assigned families to four conditions: FET with intake assessment, FET without intake assessment, minimum contact control with intake assessment, and minimum contact control without intake assessment. For this study, families in all four conditions were assessed with the SFSR at termination. Families in two conditions were assessed with the SFSR at intake but not in the remaining two conditions, in order to determine the effects of testing. The results of the study indicated that families in the FET modality showed family functioning improvement as measured by the SFSR, whereas families in the minimum contact control condition did not show improvement, and these differences between the FET and control conditions were significant. Thus once more in this study the SFSR demonstrated that it is sensitive to treatment changes in the structural condition while discriminating, as expected, between the structural and the control condition. Moreover, the results indicated that there were no effects for testing, thereby demonstrating that the SFSR is an unobtrusive measure.

The theoretical concepts and clinical strategies presented in this book have been subjected to over 10 years of rigorous research. The treatment, engagement, and diagnostic strategies that we have developed have fared extremely well when submitted to scientific scrutiny. It is for this reason that we now feel ready to share our work for other use to the clinical community.

Epilogue

In this book we have reviewed theory, application, and finally, research. Throughout the entire course of our work, we have striven to integrate all three. Structural systems theory is the foundation from which our breakthroughs in assessment, engagement, and treatment were developed. Although we have only introduced our research at the end, research has played an integral part in achieving the breakthroughs that we have described in this book. Research is both a final step in the completion of each stage of knowledge development and a solid foundation from which to pursue new breakthroughs. For example, the development of SFSR enabled us to evaluate the effectiveness of structural family therapy in a way that is immensely relevant to structural family theory and therapy. After all, structuralists are immensely interested in structural change. The clarification of the basic BSFT strategies and goals enabled us to understand how to modify these strategies to achieve the same goals without having the entire family in therapy, thus making OPFT possible. These breakthroughs that enabled us to change family interactions by working primarily through one person became, in turn, the foundation of our breakthrough in engaging resistant families in treatment: In engaging resistant families, because the therapist initially has only one person with whom to work, OPFT strategies are necessary for restructuring those family interactions keeping the family from getting treatment.

Work with families has also become the foundation for applications of structural systems theory to systems other than families. The family represents a natural system, with all the properties and characteristics of any interpersonal system. The family, however, distinguishes itself by being a small enough natural system to allow us to bring it into the "laboratory" for meticulous study. It thus becomes the prototype system for learning about all interpersonal systems.

After having learned from families how to understand and change them using concepts of systems (i.e., interdependence) and structure (i.e., patterns of interaction), we have ventured to apply these same concepts to larger systems such as organizations (Szapocznik, Blaney, Foote, & Rodriguez, in press) and communities. Thus the principles of system and structure that have been presented in this book have broad applicability to other, larger systems.

References

Coleman, S. B., & Davis, D. I. (1978). Family therapy and drug abuse: A national survey. *Family Process, 17,* 21-29.

Haley, J. (1976). *Problem-solving therapy.* San Francisco: Jossey-Bass.

Jessor, R. (1985). Adolescent problem drinking: Psychosocial aspects and development outcomes. In L. H. Towle (Ed.), *Proceedings: NIAAA-World Health Organization Collaborating Center Designation Meeting & Alcohol Seminar* (DHHS Publication No. ADM 85-1370, pp. 104-143). Rockville, MD: NIAAA.

Jessor, R., & Jessor, S. L. (1977). *Problem behavior and psychosocial development: A longitudinal study of youth.* New York: Academic Press.

Madanes, C. (1981). *Strategic family therapy.* San Francisco: Jossey-Bass.

Minuchin, S. (1974). *Families and family therapy.* Cambridge, MA: Harvard University Press.

Minuchin, S., & Fishman, H. C. (1981). *Family therapy techniques.* Cambridge, MA: Harvard University Press.

Rosman, B. (1976). *Personal communication.*

Stanton, M. D. (1979). Family treatment of drug problems: A review. In R. L. Dupont, A. Goldstein, & J. O'Donnell (Eds.), *Handbook of drug abuse.* Washington, DC: U.S. Government Printing Office.

Stanton, M. D., & Todd, T. C. (1981). Engaging resistant families in treatment. *Family Process, 20,* 261-293.

Szapocznik, J., Blaney, N., Foote, F., & Rodriguez, A. (in press). A strategic structural systems approach to organizational change and institutional racism. In L. J. Duhl (Ed.), *The urban condition II.* New York: Springer.

Szapocznik, J., Foote, F., Perez-Vidal, A., Hervis, O., & Kurtines, W. (1985). *One person family therapy.* Miami: Miami World Health Organization Collaborating Center for Research and Training in Mental Health, Alcohol and Drug Dependence, Department of Psychiatry, University of Miami School of Medicine.

Szapocznik, J., Hervis, O., Rio, A., Faraci, A. M., Murray, E., & Kurtines, W. (under editorial review). *The structural family systems ratings: An interactional measure of family functioning.*

Szapocznik, J., Kurtines, W. M., Foote, F., Perez-Vidal, A., & Hervis, O. (1983). Conjoint versus one person family therapy: Some evidence for the effectiveness of conducting family therapy through one person. *Journal of Consulting and Clinical Psychology, 51,* 889–899.

Szapocznik, J., Kurtines, W. M., Foote, F., Perez-Vidal, A., & Hervis, O. (1986). Conjoint versus one person family therapy: Further evidence for the effectiveness of conducting family therapy through one person. *Journal of Consulting and Clinical Psychology, 54,* 395–397.

Szapocznik, J., Kurtines, W., Perez-Vidal, A., Hervis, O., & Foote, F. (in press). One person family therapy. In R. A. Wells & V. J. Giannetti (Eds.), *Handbook of brief psychotherapies.* New York: Plenum.

Szapocznik, J., Perez-Vidal, A., Brickman, A., Foote, F. H., Santisteban, D., Hervis, O., & Kurtines, W. M. (1989). Engaging adolescent drug abusers and their families into treatment: A strategic structural systems approach. *Journal of Consulting and Clinical Psychology, 56,* 552–557.

Szapocznik, J., Perez-Vidal, A., Brickman, A., Kurtines, W., Foote, F., Hervis, O., & Santisteban, D. (1987). *Structural family systems engagement of adolescent drug abusers: Final report* (NIDA Grant No. R18 DA03224). Miami: University of Miami Spanish Family Guidance Center.

Szapocznik, J., Perez-Vidal A., Hervis, O., Brickman, A. L., & Kurtines, W. A. (in press). Innovations in family therapy: Strategies for overcoming resistance to treatment. In R. A. Wells & V. J. Giannetti (Eds.), *Handbook of brief psychotherapies.* New York: Plenum.

Szapocznik, J., Perez-Vidal, A., Hervis, O., Foote, F., & Kurtines, W. (1986). Terapia de familia a traves de un solo miembro: FamUno. *Cuadernos de Psiocologia, 8,* 53–80.

Szapocznik, J., Perez-Vidal, A., Hervis, O., Foote, F., & Spencer, F. (1983). *Brief strategic family therapy: Final report* (NIDA Grant No. R18 DA03224). Miami: University of Miami Spanish Family Guidance Center.

Szapocznik, J., Rio, A., Cohen, R., Hervis, O., Murray, E., Posada, V., Santisteban, D., Scopetta, M., & Rivas-Vasquez, A. (1987). *Psychodynamic and structural treatment for hispanic children: Final report* (NIMH Grant No. 1-R01-MH34821). Miami: University of Miami.

Szapocznik, J., Rio, A., Murray, E., Cohen, R., Scopetta, M., Revis-Vasquez, A., Hervis, O., Posada, V., & Kurtines, W. (in press). Structural family versus psychodynamic child therapy for problematic Hispanic boys. *Journal of Consulting and Clinical Psychology.*

Szapocznik, J., Rio, A., Perez-Vidal, A., Kurtines, W., & Santisteban, D. (1984).

Family effectiveness training: Final report (NIDA Grant No. 02694). Miami: University of Miami Spanish Family Guidance Center.

Szapocznik, J., Santisteban, D., Kurtines, W. M., Perez-Vidal, A., & Hervis, O. (1984). Bicultural effectiveness training: A treatment intervention for enhancing intercultural adjustment. *Hispanic Journal of Behavioral Sciences, 6,* 317–344.

Szapocznik, J., Santisteban, D., Rio, A., Perez-Vidal, A., Kurtines, W., & Hervis, O. (1986). Bicultural effectiveness training (BET): An intervention modality for families experiencing intergenerational/intercultural conflict. *Hispanic Journal of Behavioral Sciences, 6,* 303–330.

Szapocznik, J., Santisteban, D., Rio, A., Perez-Vidal, A., Santisteban, D. (in press). Family effectiveness training: An intervention to prevent problem behavior in hispanic adolescents. *Hispanic Journal of Behavioral Sciences.*

Appendix

Structural Family Systems Rating Form

RATING FORM

Structural Family Systems Ratings

Project —————————

Case No. ————————— Date Rating Done —————————

Date of administration: —————————

Rater's Name —————————

Comments —————————

—————————

—————————

—————————

Members Present (circle)

IP	Mo
Fa	C2
C3	C4
GM	GF
Other —————	

Structure	Flexibility	Resonance	Developmental Stage	Identified Patienthood	Conflict Resolution	I	T	F-U

A. Structure
  1. Leadership _____

    (List all who assume leadership. Is it shared? Is it balanced? Is it appropriate?)

    (a) Hierarchy _____

      (List pecking order. Is it appropriate?)
    (b) Behavior control _____

      (Who disciplines? Who keeps individuals on task? Are they the appropriate people?)
    (c) Guidance _____

      (Who gives it? Is it appropriately used?)
  2. Subsystem organization _____

    (List existing subsystems. Are they well defined? Are some appropriate subsystems missing?)
    (a) Alliances _____

      (Who sides with whom? Do they follow along subsystem lines? Are they appropriate?)
    (b) Triangulations _____

      (Is a third party unnecessarily involved in a dyad? If so, who, which dyad(s), and how often?)
    (c) Subsystem membership _____

      (Who is a member of which sybsystem? Are subsystems appropriate as to age and function? Are subsystem barriers strong?)
  3. Communication flow _____

    (List all possible dyads—e.g., Mo-IP, C2-C3, etc.—and indicate whether communication in each dyad occurs frequently, sometimes, rarely, or never.)
    (a) Directness of communication _____

      (Is communication clear and direct between individuals and subsystems?)

(b) Gatekeepers/switchboard operators _____

_____

(List any that exist.)
(c) Spokesperson _____
(List any that exist.)

Each major dimension (leadership, subsystem organization, and communication flow) has three subheadings. The rater places a check mark under each subheading whenever a dysfunctional behavior is observed. A dimension is rated "excellent" if there are no check marks assigned to the three subheadings. An "average" rating is given to a family with only one check in each respective dimension. A "dysfunctional" rating is assigned to a family who has been assigned at least two checks per category.

	Excellent (no checks)	*Average* (one check)	*Dysfunctional* (two or more checks)
Leadership (L)	3	2	0
Subsystem Organization (S.O.)	3	2	0
Communication Flow (C.F.)	3	2	0

Total = _____ + _____ + _____ = _____

Structure Rating (circle one)   L   S.O.   C.F.   Total

1. *Very dysfunctional structure* (score 0)
   Family structure clearly very unhealthy. All major dimensions are dysfunctional.
2. *Dysfunctional structure* (score 2)
   Family structure not generally healthy. Two of the three major dimensions are dysfunctional, and the third is only average.
3. *Average structure* (scores 4-5)
   Generally healthy family structure but with at least one major dimension flaw.
4. *Good structure* (scores 6-7)
   Generally healthy family structure with minor flaws that do not seriously impede family functioning.
5. *Excellent structure* (scores 8-9)
   Very healthy family structure with at least two of the three major dimensions functioning at an excellent level and the other at an average level at all times.

B. Flexibility
   Score each one of the below that occurs:
   1. *Shifts in communication flow*: _____
   _____

   2. *Alliance shifts*: _____
   _____

   3. *Subsystem formation changes*: _____
   _____

   4. *Shifts in ways of resolving conflict*: _____
   _____

   5. *Shifts in organization from task to task*: _____
   _____

The rating is obtained by dividing the number of appropriate shifts by the total number of shifts for each of the three family tasks.

Flexibility Rating (circle one)
   1. *Very rigid system*
      Appropriate shifts occur successfully less than 25% of the time. Little if any shifting in alliance, subsystems, or communication flow patterns. Conflict resolution style is always denial or avoidance.
   2. *Moderately rigid system*
      Appropriate shifts occur unsuccessfully at least 25% of the time but less than 50% of the time. One or two shifts occur in more than two of the five categories above. These shifts are appropriate to structure and stimuli. Major dysfunctional coalitions remain rigid.
   3. *Somewhat flexible system*
      Appropriate shifts occur successfully at least 50% of the time but less than 75% of the time. Three or four shifts occur in at least two of the five categories above. Some major coalitions or communication pathways or conflict style remain rigid; others change.
   4. *Moderately flexible system*
      Appropriate shifts occur successfully at least 75% of the time but less than 90% of the time. Shifting occurs at least five times in at least three of the five categories above. Only one flaw in alliance rigidity, communication flow, or conflict resolution style remains fixed throughout.
   5. *Very flexible system*
      Appropriate shifts occur at least 90% of the time. Shifting occurs more than five times and is evident on all five categories above and is appropriately responsive to stimuli and to healthy structure. Patterns of conflict resolution do not stay fixed in denial or avoidance; alliances are rediffused according to the issue involved.

C. Resonance

The following are scored each time the event occurs in Tasks I and II:

1. Mind readings _____
   (A tells others what B believes, wants, or feels without B expressing an opinion.)
2. Mediated responses _____
   (A tells or asks C about something B said.)
3. Differentiated responses _____
   (An individual is spoken about in unambiguous and somewhat unique terms.)
4. Semidifferentiated responses _____
   (A subgrouping of family members is referred to and/or content is somewhat ambiguous.)
5. Undifferentiated responses _____
   (Family members are referred to as a class or a part of a larger group.)
6. Simultaneous speeches _____
   (Two or more people talk at the same time for at least 5 sec.)
7. Interruptions _____
   (One person breaks into and stops another's speech and takes off on a different train of thought.)
8. Continuations _____
   (One person breaks into another's speech but retains some of the original speaker meaning.)
9. Person control _____
   (A speaks authoritatively about B to C, implying special knowledge and/or control of B.)
10. Loss of distance _____
    (Two or more people touch each other or get very close to each other.)
11. Joint affective reaction _____
    (Crying together, laughing together, or other nonverbal joint affective response.)
12. Engagement reaction _____
    (Chain of interchanges that spreads from one dyad to another.)

Resonance Rating (circle one)

1. Nonexistent or impermeable boundaries
   Very enmeshed and/or disengaged system
   (a) Many of #1 through #12 above (except for #3) and no differentiated responses.
   (b) No #6–#12 and no alliances noted.

2. Poorly defined or slightly permeable boundaries
   Moderately enmeshed and/or disengaged system
   (a) Many mind readings, mediated responses, and global responses; some of the rest (1 through 12 except for #3) and none or very few differentiated responses.
   (b) Very few #6s, #7s, #8s, #9s, #10s, #11s, #12s (just one or two of these), while only one alliance is noted.

3. Somewhat defined and/or somewhat permeable boundaries
   Somewhat enmeshed and/or disengaged system
   (a) very few mind readings, mediated responses, and global responses; very few of the rest of #s 1–12 (except for #3) and very few (one or two) differentiated responses.
   (b) Alliances are evident. There are a very few of #s 1–12; communication flows among all members, but there is very little affection noted from one to another.

4. Moderately well defined yet permeable boundaries
   Slightly enmeshed and/or disengaged system
   (a) Some #s 4–12 but they never disrupt appropriate structure. No #s 1–2. Several (three or four) differentiated responses.
   (b) Interaction is effective.

5. Well defined yet permeable boundaries
   Not enmeshed and/or disengaged system
   (a) No #s 1–2.
   (b) Minimal #4–12.
   (c) Many (five or more) differentiated responses.
   (d) Alliances good.
   (e) Affective responses among all members.
   (f) Communication flows freely among all.

D. Developmental Stage
   Score a check in subheading when dysfunction is observed: Check overall task and roles as dysfunctional.
   1. *Parenting tasks and roles*: (circle one: *f*unctional or *d*ysfunctional)   f   d
      (a) Competence _____
      (b) Unsuccessful leadership _____
      (c) Nurturance _____
   2. *Spousal tasks and roles*:   f   d
      (a) Parent supports child against spouse _____
      (b) Parent elicits protective support from child _____

      (c) Spouse fails to support other spouse when needed?

3. *Sibling tasks and roles:*   f   d
   (a) Age-appropriate child competence? _____
       Child's rights at age level? _____
4. *Extended family tasks and roles:*   f   d
   (a) Parents in proper position vis-à-vis grandparents or
       other kin? _____
   (b) Parental authority delegated appropriately, *not*
       usurped? _____

Developmental Stage Rating (circle one)
   1. *Very dysfunctional developmental performance*
      All three tasks and role scales (or all four if extended family)
      have been rated dysfunctional and six subheadings have at least
      one incident of dysfunctionality.
   2. *Dysfunctional developmental performance*
      Two task and role scales have been rated dysfunctional.
   3. *Somewhat attenuated developmental performance*
      One task and role scale has been rated dysfunctional.
   4. *Good developmental performance*
      No role scale has been rated dysfunctional but up to two of the
      subheadings do have at least one incident of dysfunctionality.
   5. *Excellent developmental performance*
      There are no checks in subheadings, and all task and role scales
      are rated functional.
E. Identified Patienthood
   1. Negativity about the IP _____
      (IP is seen as cause of family pain and unhappiness.)
   2. IP centrality _____
      (IP is center of attention or topic of conversation—does not
      count as symptom unless occurs three or more times, excluding
      minimal requirements for task two.)
   3. Overprotection of IPhood _____
      (Confrontation of IP dysfunction is avoided by minimization,
      making excuses, etc.)
   4. Nurturance of IPhood _____
      (IP dysfunction is supported or abetted by other family
      members.)
   5. Denial of other problems _____
      (Statements are made reflecting both that the IP causes pain/
      unhappiness *and* that the family has no other problems.)
   6. Other IPhood _____
      (Negative statements about family member other than the IP, or
      references to the problematic nature of the behavior of another

family member, or the identification of other problems of the IP different than the presenting complaint.)

Identified Patienthood Rating (circle one)
1. *Very rigid Iphood*
   At least four of #1–5 above are present but Other IP(#6) is not present.
2. *Moderately rigid Iphood*
   Two or three of #1–5 above are present and Other IP(#6) is not present *or* all of #1–6 are present.
3. *Somewhat flexible IPhood*
   Two, three, or four of #1–5 above are present and Other IP(#6) is also clearly present.
4. *Moderately flexible IPhood*
   One of #1–5 above is present. Other IP(#6) may or may not be present.
5. *Very flexible IPhood*
   None of #1–5 is present. Other IP(#6) may or may not be present.

F. Conflict Resolution
1. Denial _____
   (Conflict is not allowed to emerge.)
2. Avoidance _____
   (Conflict begins to emerge but is stopped, masked, or strongly inhibited.)
3. Diffusion _____
   (Keeping system in conflict but avoiding or sabotaging clear emergence and confrontation.)
4. Emergence without resolution _____
   (Differing opinions expressed and confronted, but no one solution finally accepted.)
5. Emergence with resolution _____
   (Differing opinions expressed and confronted, with one solution acceptable to all finally found.)

Number of denials .... _____ ..... × 0 = _____
Number of avoidances .... _____ ..... × 1 = _____
Number of diffusions .... _____ ..... × 2 = _____
Number of emergence without
  resolution .... _____ ..... × 3 = _____
Number of emergence with
  resolution .... _____ ..... × 5 = _____
(Sum) Total number of conflicts .... _____
　　　　　　　　　　　　(Sum) Total conflict score ...... _____
Total conflict score/total number of conflicts =
_____ weighted average conflict score.

Conflict Resolution Rating (circle one)
1. *Very poor handling of conflicts*
   Weighted average conflict score: 0–1.50
2. *Poor handling of conflicts*
   Weighted average conflict score: 1.51–2.50
3. *Moderate handling of conflict*
   Weighted average conflict score: 2.51–3.50
4. *Good handling of conflicts*
   Weighted average conflict score: 3.51–4.50
5. *Excellent handling of conflicts*
   Weighted average conflict score: 4.51

Index

Index